What Others Are Saying About This Book:

"This outstanding guide could have been titl
the Real Ozarks For Less Than Twenty-five 1
Complete with driving instructions, meal sto
attractions and historical highlights, it has no
tor, tour guide, or Bransonite wanting to kn
behind local sites and traditions should be wit

—*S. Burkett Milner*
president of the National To

"This enchanting book goes beyond the ex;
reader seeking a mere travel guide. It is lovingly
would write about one's own family members. The great detail
concerning routes, travel tips, suggestions and insights of
which only a local would be aware are frosted with an icing
of warm descriptive passages and generously spiced with pictures that look like they have been donated from the family
photo albums of all the original settlers of the area.

"Even if one were not planning a trip to this area, one can
enjoy this book on its own merits as a fascinating view of the
history, people and geography of one of the original garden
spots of the United States. It is a book you will thoroughly
enjoy reading. But if you intend to travel in the area, you will
find this an invaluable reference from which to plan your trip
and to take with you as your personal guide."

—*Barry Stier, president, Oceanco Ltd. Publisher of*
travel books, newspapers and magazines worldwide

"For first time visitors to Branson, seasoned regulars, and
armchair travelers alike, *Branson's Best Day Trips* is a wonderful read. I consider it one of the best local guidebooks to
any area I have ever come across. If you are planning a trip
to Branson this year, read this book first! Then bring it along

as a handy reference as you explore all the best the Branson area has to offer." —*Gypsy Journal*

"From the internationally famous tourist attractions to unforgettable, inexpensive, 'visitor friendly' out-of-the-way places only a local would know, *Branson's Best Day Trips* lives up to its title. Shaffer has enhanced this terrific guide-book with glimpses of the area's colorful past. If you are planning a Branson vacation or simply passing through, an out-of-state tourist or a Missouri native looking for something fun to do or interesting to see, begin by a careful browsing of Carol Shaffer's *Branson's Best Day Trips*."
—*Midwest Book Review*

"Now *this* is a guidebook, written by 'local' Carol Shaffer. The book mixes area history (better than any show!) and photographs with a complete guide to Ozark attractions from local theme parks to inexpensive day trips in the area. To help you get there, she has also provided 18 maps and detailed directions clear enough for even the most directionally impaired traveler! To top it all off, Ms. Shaffer's writing is delightful! We recommend this book highly."
—*Fairfield/Branson Book Review*

A Guide to Discovering the Best of Branson & Ozark Mountain Country

2nd Edition

Carol A. Shaffer

PELICAN PUBLISHING COMPANY

Gretna 2002

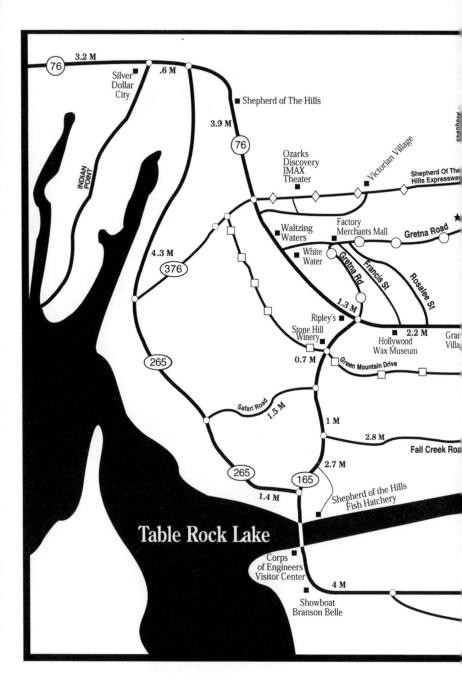

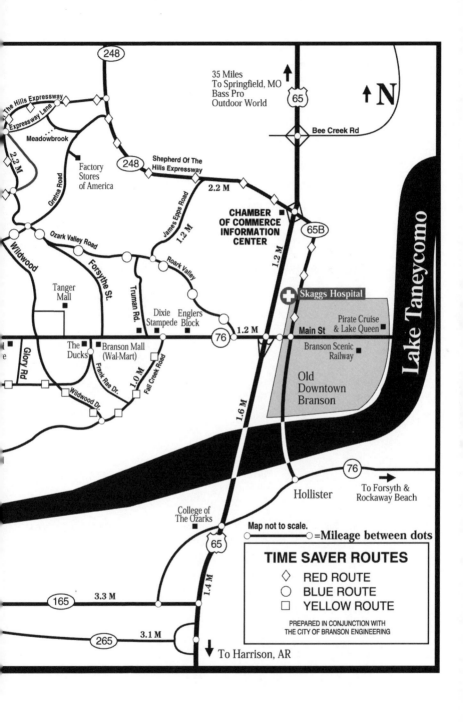

Copyright © 2000, 2002
By Carol A. Shaffer
All rights reserved

First edition, 2000
First Pelican edition, 2002

Library of Congress Cataloging-in-Publication Data

Shaffer, Carol A.
  Branson's best day trips: a guide to discovering the best of
Branson & Ozark Mountain country/Carol Shaffer.—2nd ed., 1st
Pelican ed.
    p. cm.
  Includes index.
  ISBN 1-58980-009-5 (pbk.)
  1. Branson Region (Mo.)—Tours. 2. Ozark Mountains Region—
Tours. I. Title.

F474.B79 S53 2002
977.8'797—dc21

                                     2001052312

Cover design by Mike Sears

Printed in the United States of America
Published by Pelican Publishing Company, Inc.
1000 Burmaster Street, Gretna, Louisiana 70053

Contents

Introduction

Maps

Introduction

When my husband and I moved to Branson in 1993, we wanted to learn all there was to know about our new hometown and the surrounding Ozark Mountains. After spending many weekends putting hundreds of miles on our van, we discovered so many beautiful and unusual places—both in Branson and beyond—that we wanted to share them with everyone.

Since cost is important, all of the day trips in this guide were designed with a budget in mind. Take Chapter Five, *Branson's Free Attractions*. For roughly the cost of a gallon of gasoline you can: visit a working gristmill; view two local history films; tour a fish hatchery; take a nature hike; and browse a country-style flea market and craft village. For the other trips, we quote all admission charges so that you can make your budget decisions before pulling off the roadway. In fact, every trip in this book is so packed with activities that you can easily skip one and still have a fun-filled day.

Afraid that you won't be able to find your way? Don't be! Each trip has its own map plus turn-by-turn directions. And if these directions are too detailed for some of you, please remember that we also wrote this book for Aunt Ida from Illinois. She's never driven in these tricky Ozark hills and has a frightful fear of getting lost.

While traveling through this beautiful country, you may find yourself wondering what life was like in the past. To make your trip to the colorful Ozarks more memorable, we've included some local history—no long history lessons, just the highlights. You will, for instance, discover how Branson, Missouri (pop. 3706) became, according to Morley Safer of CBS' *Sixty Minutes*, the music show capital of the universe. And why a novel written at the turn of the 20th century altered the destiny of the entire region.

To determine which day trips are best for you, here's a quick summary.

- Chapter One, *Getting Around Town*, provides maps and directions on navigating the area's confusing road system, including the newer Time Saver Routes. You'll also find directions to the Branson/Lakes Area Chamber of Commerce, source of information on everything from music shows and attractions to restaurants and lodging.

- Chapter Two explores historic *Oldtown Branson*. Attractions are lake cruises, a train ride in the Missouri and Arkansas Ozarks, wonderful eating experiences, and unique shopping—all in a setting right out of a Norman Rockwell painting!

- Chapters Three and Four cover the area's two celebrated theme parks, *Shepherd of the Hills Homestead* and *Silver Dollar City*. In 1998 Silver Dollar City was named the world's best theme park by the International Association of Amusement Parks and Attractions. Although the parks charge admission fees, both offer a taste of Branson and the Ozarks that's impossible to match.

- Chapter Five deals with Branson's *Free Attractions*. Highlights include a working gristmill at the College of the Ozarks, Table Rock Dam, two local history films, two nature hikes, shopping, and fantastic scenery.

- When you're ready to venture away from town, the two trips in Chapter Six, *Nearby Historic Towns*, will guide you through the hills and hollows to communities within fifteen miles of Branson. Flea market fans will especially enjoy the trip to Reeds Spring and Branson West, and history buffs the one to Rockaway Beach, Forsyth, and Hollister. Scenery aficionados will love them both.

- Can't get enough Victorian-style architecture? If so, you won't want to miss the nostalgic trip in Chapter Seven to *Enchanting Eureka Springs*. Attractions are a trolley ride down streets lined with Victorian homes, and a stroll through the city's historical downtown district crowded with over a hundred shops and art galleries.

- Chapter Eight's main attraction is Bass Pro Shops Outdoor World in *Springfield, Missouri*. Bass Pro—Missouri's most visited attraction—is more than a sporting goods store; it's an adventure. This day trip includes a driving tour of a Civil War battlefield, a fantastic wildlife museum, a cave where you ride a tram rather than walk, and a gem of a wild animal park.

- If you love nature and nostalgic settings, check out *Ozarks Outdoors* in Chapter Nine. You'll visit pretty Roaring River State Park with its trout stream, fish hatchery, and hiking trails; a Civil War battlefield; and picturesque War Eagle Mill.

- For the more adventurous, there's *Off the Beaten Path* in Chapter Ten. This day trip offers the option of touring a cave and pioneer museum before working off some vacation calories by hiking two wilderness trails in the Buffalo National River Park in Arkansas. The full day of outdoor activities will end with dinner overlooking the spectacular Grand Canyon of the Ozarks.

- The last and longest day trip is *Points North* in Chapter Eleven. In historic Carthage, Missouri, is the beautiful Precious Moments Chapel designed by Samuel J. Butcher, creator of the popular Precious Moments figurines.

Okay! It's time to get behind the wheel and start exploring everything that Branson and the rest of Ozark Mountain Country has to offer. Nothing has been left to chance—you'll know where to go, what to see and do, and what it's going to cost. Your vacation to the Ozarks—rich in history and blessed by Mother Nature—is guaranteed to be one of the most entertaining ever!

Note: When you see the following symbol, you'll know it's time to head for the car and travel to the next attraction.

The man who goes alone can start today, but he who travels with another must wait until that other is ready.

—Henry David Thoreau

Inspiration Tower at Shepherd of the Hills Homestead.

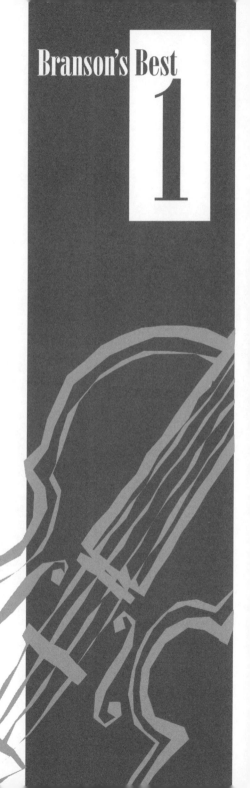

Getting

Around

Town

Where to Go First

What to See First

**The Indispensable
Time Saver Routes**

1

Welcome to Branson!

Where To Go First

After you get to town, the first order of the day is to pay a visit to the **Branson Chamber of Commerce Tourist Information Center.** The always-friendly staff is just waiting to welcome visitors, so be sure to stop in for a cup of coffee and some old-fashioned Ozark hospitality.

> **Branson/Lakes Area Chamber of Commerce and Convention and Visitor Bureau**
> (800) 961-1221 or (417) 334-4136
> Monday through Friday, 8 A.M. to 6 P.M.; Saturday, 8 A.M. to 5 P.M., Sunday, 10 A.M. to 4 P.M.
> Web site: www.bransonchamber.com

Branson/Lakes Area Chamber of Commerce.

The Information Center is conveniently located on the southwest corner of **U.S. 65** and **Missouri 248 (Shepherd of the Hills Expressway/Veterans Blvd)**. *See Red Time Saver Route in this chapter for details.*

If you're coming from Springfield on U.S. 65, exit at Missouri 248 and turn right. Turn left at the first driveway (by the big blue Tourist Information sign). If you're coming from Arkansas on U.S. 65, travel one mile past Missouri 76 to Missouri 248 (exiting right), travel to the stoplight and turn left, crossing over U.S. 65. The Information Center is immediately on your left.

Information On Everything

Sitting in middle of the Visitor Center lobby is a huge kiosk filled with hundreds of brochures detailing music shows, lodging facilities, and area attractions. Now's the time to pick up additional information to help you decide what you would most like to see and do. Be sure to look for a current *Branson Show Guide,* or ask for one at the front desk.

Area Maps

Be sure to ask at the desk for a copy of the *Branson Roads Scholar.* The brochure's color-coded map will help you find your way on the town's three Time Saver Routes. *Detailed information about these color-coded routes is given later in this chapter.*

Free Publications

Lining the wall near the entrance are racks displaying free

publications. Pick up copies of: *Best Read Guide* (has a complete theater listing including prices); *Happy Camper* (has a good color map); *Sunny Day Guide; Branson This Week; Ozark Mountain Visitor; Restaurant Entertainment Guide;* and any others that happen to be there. All have money-saving coupons for restaurants and attractions.

Lodging Reservations

If you're in need of a place to stay, ask one of the staff about the **Lodging Locator**—a computerized listing of motels and resorts with current available accommodations. If you need help operating the computer, don't hesitate to ask for help. There's no charge for this service.

What To See First

The first thing you'll probably want to see is "the town." U.S. 65 (running north and south) divides Branson into two parts: the old historical waterfront and downtown section, and the newer theater-studded district. If you look at the two-page map in the front, you'll see that the street running east and west through both is **Missouri 76,** also known as **76 Country Boulevard** or "**the Strip**." The Strip is about five miles of restaurants, motels, theaters, miniature golf courses and gift shops. During certain times of the day, traffic along the Strip can be traffic from the netherworld.

Traffic Woes

If Branson's early planners had possessed a crystal ball, they would have built W. Missouri 76 with five lanes. But there wasn't any crystal ball, and the town slowly expanded through the years along a two-lane roadway. Since 1987 Branson has seen such phenomenal growth that it has been impossible to predict what to expect from one year to the next. In 1993 alone the city issued permits for $139 million in new construction.

How to keep traffic moving is the city's highest priority. Looking at a city map, you might say, "They just need to build a few more roads." Well, roads are being built, but one look to the right and left of W. Missouri 76 will illustrate why it's lots easier said than done. The beautiful hills and valleys (one of the reasons we all love the area so much) create obstacles that require plenty of time and money to overcome.

The State of Missouri, Taney County, and the City of Branson are working hard to resolve the traffic problem. Many new roads have been built and more are in the planning stages. Also, new attractions and theaters are being built on the secondary roads to help alleviate traffic headaches on the Strip.

For now, your best bet is to study the road system and learn the Time Saver Routes and the best times of the day to travel on the Strip.

The Bright Side

Sometimes traveling slowly isn't so bad; it gives you a chance to get a good look at places you may want to visit later. One helpful Branson phenomenon is the drive-friendly attitude. You'll find motorists all over town giving the right of way to other drivers. Since we're all in this together, pass it on and give the other guy a break whenever you can.

The Indispensable Time Saver Routes

Local residents can go anywhere they want on the Strip without spending any appreciable time sitting in traffic. You can do it too, if you learn the Time Saver Routes and use them every chance you get. These alternate routes will get you to the theater in time for the show and—what's more important—keep your temper from reaching the boiling point.

Time Saving Tips!

- Schedule shopping and sightseeing trips for less busy times of day. From Labor Day to Memorial Day, and during the month of October, the Strip really gets packed after 9:30 A.M. (when everyone is coming into town), and before and after the afternoon and evening music shows.
- Plan an entire day's activities so you won't waste time going back and forth to your motel.
- Learn the Time Saver Routes.
- Use the Time Saver Routes!

Branson has three color-coded Time Saver Routes. The **Red** and **Blue Routes** parallel the Strip to the north, and the **Yellow Route** parallels it to the south. Symbols in the designated colors are painted periodically on the pavement along each route.

Traffic is usually light on these routes (except at some of the intersections), so take the time to find them as soon as you get to Branson—it will be worth it!

The Red Route

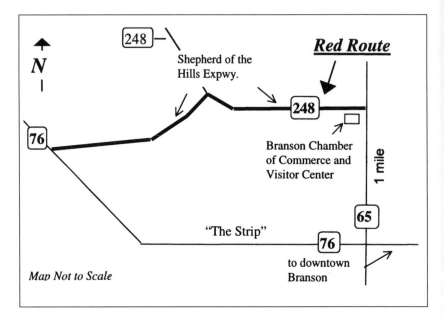

This route parallels the Strip north of Branson before it heads south and connects with it at its west end. To follow the Red Route from the **U.S. 65/Missouri 76** intersection, travel one mile north to **Missouri 248/Shepherd of the Hills Expressway.** Exit to the right and travel to the stoplight (staying in the left lane). Turn left, heading west on Missouri 248. Travel 2 miles to where the Expressway leaves 248 and takes off to the left. Follow the Expressway (about 3.5 miles) to **W. Missouri 76.** Two roads, **James F. Epps** (by Kmart) and a recently built extension of **Gretna**, go off from Missouri 248 and connect with **Roark Valley Road** and the **Blue Route** (see Blue Route map).

This route is a combination of **Roark Valley Road** and **Gretna Road.** Like the Red Route, it parallels the Strip to the north. Several roads take off from Roark and Gretna (like spokes in a wheel), returning to the Strip at various points.

The Blue Route

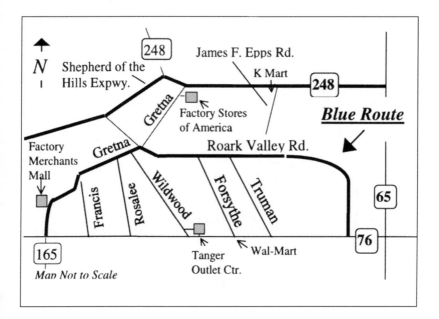

To follow the Blue Route from the **U.S. 65/Missouri 76 intersection,** travel west on Missouri 76, staying in the right lane as you head up the hill (you'll enjoy bypassing all those people in the center lane who aren't aware of the Blue Route). At the stoplight, turn right onto Roark Valley Road. Roark Valley will head north and then curve west, paralleling the Strip. Along Roark Valley, **Truman Drive** and **Forsythe St.** will take off to the south and head back to the Strip. (Forsythe will take you back to 76 near Wal-Mart.)

To complete the Blue Route, continue following Roark to Gretna Road and turn left. Gretna will take you back to the Strip. **Wildwood Drive, Rosalee** and **Francis** all take off from Gretna and return to the Strip. The **Factory Merchants Mall** (look for the big red roof) is located on this section of Gretna.

Gretna Road ends at Missouri 76. If you cross 76 at the

intersection, the road on the south side becomes Missouri 165 and eventually circles east (about 12 miles) and connects with U.S. 65 about 3 miles south of Branson. There are lots of free attractions and beautiful scenery along Missouri 165—*see Chapter Five for a guided tour.*

The Yellow Route

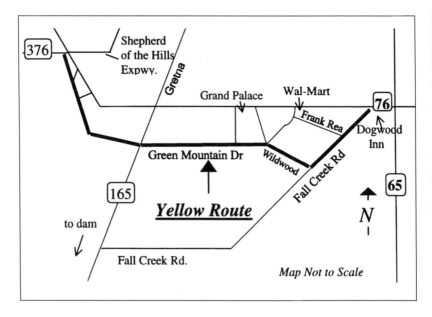

To follow the Yellow Route from the **U.S. 65/Missouri 76** intersection, travel west on Missouri 76 for 1.2 miles to **Fall Creek Road** (by the Dogwood Inn). Turn left on Fall Creek and follow it past **Frank Rea Boulevard** (this road will take you to the back of Wal-Mart) to **Wildwood Drive.** Turn right and follow Wildwood to **Green Mountain Drive.** Turn left (you'll be behind the Grand Palace) and follow Green Mountain to Missouri 165. If you turn right on Missouri 165, you'll head back to the Strip. If you turn left, you'll be heading south toward the Shepherd of the Hills Hatchery and Table Rock Dam.

If you stay on Green Mountain Dr., it will take you behind several theaters and connect with **Missouri 376** at the west end of the Strip.

Remember, Branson is a small town filled with friendly people—glad to be here and glad you came to visit. If you should get lost, you won't be far off course, and local folks are always happy to steer you in the right direction.

The traffic flow in Branson has improved greatly, thanks to the addition of the recently completed Time Saver Routes.

Oldtown Branson:

Yesterday & Today

Shopping

Dining

Lake Taneycomo

History of Branson

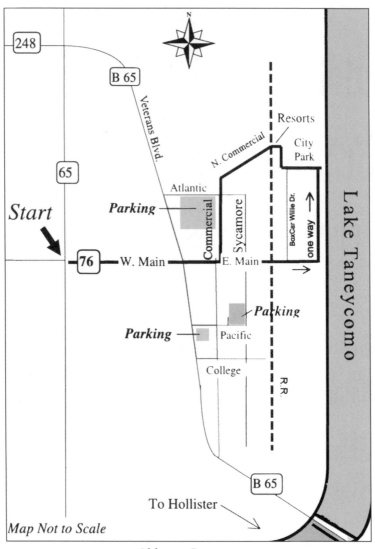

Oldtown Branson.

Unlike the rainbow-hued neon look of the Strip, old downtown Branson reflects the gentle ways of times past. Striped awnings shade clean-swept sidewalks lined with vintage style lampposts. Shoppers amble past near century-old storefronts housing gift shops, bakeries, candy stores and hometown cafes. Down the hill, a turn-of-the-century paddlewheel docks at the foot of Main Street, and the railroad delivers passengers to a 90-year-old depot.

Shopping in the downtown district is as diverse as you'll find anywhere in the Tri-Lakes area. Retail stores overflow with an array of merchandise, from Western wear and Victorian finery to collector dolls and fine art. But don't think you've seen it all until you spend some time in the area's gigantic flea markets, crammed with thousands of old-time treasures and crafts. Allow at least half a day to wander, browse, and soak up all of downtown Branson's country-style ambiance.

How To Get There

From the **U.S. 65** and **Missouri 76** intersection, follow Missouri 76 East (also called **Main St.**) about half a mile down the hill to the downtown shopping district. Commercial activity focuses on Main St., but the town sprawls from the top of the hill down to Lake Taneycomo.

Parking

Parking is available along the main streets, but because there is a two-hour parking limit that is enforced, you're better off in one of the public lots. There are public lots north on **Commercial,** south on **Sycamore** and south on **Business 65**—see map for locations.

Shopping

The four-way stoplight at Main and Business 65 marks the beginning of the main shopping district. Shops line Main from here to the railroad tracks, north and south on Commercial St., and along Business 65. Although it would be too time-consuming to list all the shops in the downtown district, here are a few of special interest.

One fun store you shouldn't miss is **Dick's Old-time 5 & 10** (103 W. Main), in business since 1929. You'll be amazed at how they can fit so much stuff in one place. It's chock full of thousands of household items, dry goods, craft supplies, toys and souvenirs.

For Victorian finery, there's a beautifully decorated shop called **Patricia's House** (101 W. Main). The building housing Patricia's was once the town's bank, and it still has a night depository slot near the front entrance. Another beautiful shop to explore is **Ivy Rose Quilts** (118 W. Main). Ivy Rose has one of the largest selections of quilts in town.

The serious collector of vintage merchandise can browse for hours in downtown Branson's many quaint flea markets. Two of the largest located on Main are **Cadwells** (114 E. Main) and **The Flea Bag** (106 E. Main).

Commercial Street Shops

A great bargain shop worth finding is **Henry's Warehouse Outlet** (106 S. Commercial). Henry's features discount

Downtown Branson, home of the annual Old Time Fiddle Contest, is a "must see" any time of the year. *Photos courtesy of Downtown Branson Main Street Association.*

There's something for everyone at Dick's
Old-time 5 & 10 in Downtown Branson.
*Photo courtesy of Branson/Lakes Area
Chamber of Commerce.*

merchandise such as greeting cards, wrapping paper and gift
items. Stained-glass enthusiasts will be interested in
Burlington Store Annex (201 S. Commercial). It's worth the
extra steps to see all the treasures in this beautiful and unique
shop.

A historic building at 205 S. Commercial is the **Owen
Theater.** The theater, built in 1936, was the first place in the
area to show talking pictures. Jim Owen, one of Branson's
best-known entrepreneurs, built and operated the theater in
addition to running a popular resort and fishing guide service
that attracted such celebrities as Gene Autry and Charlton
Heston. The theater has many old-fashioned features such as
an outdoor ticket booth, a stone foyer and fireplace, wagon-
wheel chandeliers, and four huge murals painted by
renowned artist Elsie Bates.

Dining in Downtown Branson

The downtown district has several "country cookin' " cafes. Restaurants serving homestyle fare are: **Branson Cafe** (120 W. Main), **Farmhouse Restaurant** (119 W. Main), **The Shack Cafe** (108 N. Commercial) and **Downtown Cafe** (118 N. Commercial). All have plate lunches as well as sandwiches and burgers—look for menus and daily specials posted on storefront windows.

Authentic Italian fare (lunch specials served Monday through Saturday) is served at **Rocky's Italian Restaurant** (120 N. Sycamore, one block north of Main).

Some restaurants easy on the budget are **Mr. G's Chicago Style Pizza and Italian Food** (202 N. Commercial), **Pepper Bellies Mexican Restaurant** (305 E. Main—east of the railroad tracks), and **Dillon's Pub** (309 E. Main). Dillon's Pub, also east of the tracks, is a local hangout famous for its killer-size hamburgers.

If you have a sweet tooth, there are lots of goodies to be found. Besides the delicious pies and cobblers served at the area restaurants, other downtown shops will tempt you with fresh baked goods, ice cream treats and homemade candies. **Bekemeier's Apple Butter Shoppe and Mr. B's Ice Cream Parlor** (at the corner of Main & Business 65) specializes in fresh fruit butters—ask for a sample to find your favorite. **The Fudge Shop** (next to Bekemeier's) offers made-from-scratch fudge, taffy, and chocolates (including sugar-free varieties).

Remnants of the Past

Some of Branson's oldest buildings are located along Main St. Built in the nineteenth century, all have survived numerous floods and more than one devastating fire (a fire in 1912 destroyed twenty-one of the town's businesses). They include: **the Branson Depot,** a gift shop at 123 E. Main, the **Branson Scenic Railway Depot,** and the **Branson Hotel** at

214 W. Main (one of Branson's foremost B&Bs). Harold Bell Wright, author of *The Shepherd of the Hills,* was a frequent guest of the Branson Hotel. *See Chapter Three for a day trip to the Shepherd of the Hills Homestead, the site where Wright gained inspiration for his novel.*

The Lakefront

When you're ready to leave the shopping district and visit the lakefront, return to Main St. and follow it downhill to Lake Taneycomo. (After you cross the railroad tracks, Main St. becomes one-way.) If you're interested in a scenic excursion through the Missouri and Arkansas Ozarks, be sure to stop at the **Branson Scenic Railway Depot** (800) 2 TRAIN 2. Admission for the two-hour trip is $20.25 for adults and $10.25 for children ages three to twelve.

The Lake Queen, docked at the foot of Main St. in downtown Branson, sets sail daily on Lake Taneycomo. *Photo courtesy of the Lake Queen.*

At the turn of the twentieth century, Branson's lakefront was a bustling and busy place. But today you can stroll along the now quiet shoreline, visit the gift shops on the Lake Queen Dock, feed the ducks and geese (food can be purchased at the marinas) or just sit and take in the view. If you would enjoy a cruise on the **Lake Queen** (417) 334-3015, a genuine sternwheel paddleboat, admission is $12.95 for adults and $7.95 for children ages three to twelve. Departure times vary for the hour-and-a-half cruise. Breakfast and dinner cruises are also available. (Ask at the dock for details.) Another fun cruise is the **Sammy Lane Pirate Cruise**. The seventy-minute narrated tour features local history and an ambush by a not-so-scary Ozark pirate. Admission is $12.95 for adults and $7.95 for children three to twelve.

North Beach Park, at the far north end (past Scotty's Trout Dock), is a pretty park with picnic tables, a children's playground, public tennis courts, a barbecue pavilion, public fishing docks, and a paved pathway that lines the lake. If you have the time, take a minute to relax and enjoy the park. Romantic horse-drawn carriage rides are available on weekends during peak seasons.

Trout Fishing

Continually stocked with rainbow and brown trout by the U.S. Army Corps of Engineers, Lake Taneycomo is one of the country's top trout spots. In its July 2001 issue, *Field & Stream* magazine named Branson among its top twenty summertime fishing destinations. Here at the Taneycomo lakefront, anglers regularly catch their limit, using worms, salmon eggs, or power bait (a commercial product that comes in an array of psychedelic colors), and a simple bait-casting outfit.

If you're into fly fishing, however, you'll find better fishing conditions (when the dam isn't generating electricity) below Table Rock Dam near the Shepherd of the Hills Hatchery. *To visit the dam and hatchery, see Chapter Five—Branson's Free Attractions.*

The Branson Hotel, built in 1903, was the town's first hotel. Included in this photo, taken in 1905, is Shepherd of the Hills author Harold Bell Wright (with vest). *Photo courtesy of Marie and T.J. Stottle and Teri Murguia, current owner of the Branson Hotel.*

The marinas along the lakefront offer boats, motors, fuel, bait, tackle, and guide service. These are **Main Street Marina,** (417) 334-2263, **Branson Trout Dock,** (417) 334-3703, and **Scotty's Trout Dock,** (417) 334-4288 (Scotty's has a reasonably priced half-day group rate).

Goodbye to Yesteryear

If things go as planned, the Taneycomo lakefront may soon experience massive changes. A $300 million project has been approved, but not as yet funded, that will turn the area into one big convention center complex. Instead of old-fashioned storefronts and fishing resorts, the lakefront will be comprised of a convention center with a 10,000-seat arena, a 350-room hotel, exhibition halls, and a boardwalk lined with eclectic shops and restaurants. Construction is projected to start in 2002.

When ready to leave the lakefront, follow the street in front of the fishing docks (it will curve left). At **BoxCar Willie Drive**, turn right and follow the street as it parallels the railroad tracks (on the right is downtown Branson's main resort area). After the road curves to the left crossing the tracks, you'll be on **N. Commercial** heading back to Main Street. Just after crossing the tracks, you'll see the pretty blue-and-white **Landmark Inn,** built in 1905 to accommodate the builders of the railroad. Today the picturesque hotel is still providing low-cost lodging to Branson's visitors.

To return to your starting point, turn right at Main St. and follow it up the hill to the Missouri 76 and U.S. 65 intersection.

Branson's Fascinating History

Not long ago, Branson was just a sleepy little fishing village nestled in the Ozark hills. Tourists came mainly in the spring and summer to marvel at the spectacular Ozark scenery, shop for locally made crafts, and boat, fish and swim in the area's lakes. Many of the same families came year after year to visit the 19th century theme park called Silver Dollar City, and relive the story made famous by Harold Bell Wright at the Shepherd of the Hills Homestead. Only a handful of family-owned music shows presented weekend performances.

To see how Branson became, according to Morley Safer of CBS' Sixty Minutes, "the music-show capital of the universe," let's take a journey back in time.

The Early Years

When the first white settlers came to the Ozarks, Indians

were already hunting and fishing along the banks of the White River—the Osage tribe claims territorial rights as far back as 1673. After the Louisiana Purchase opened the territory west of the Mississippi to homesteaders in 1803, white settlers, mostly from Southern states such as North Carolina, Kentucky, Virginia and Tennessee, began staking their claim to land in the Ozarks. They chose to settle in this rugged mountain country because it reminded them of their homelands in the Appalachians. Many descendants of these original settlers still live in and around Branson.

During the Civil War, America was a country divided—and so were the people of the Ozarks. Many of the area's inhabitants sided with the North, while others supported the South. This conflict between neighbors resulted in family feuds that continued to the turn of the century and beyond.

After the war ended, outlaws and bushwhackers roamed the hills around the county seat of Forsyth (about thirteen

Branson in 1907. At center of photo is a log skid along which logs were slid to the river to be floated down to the pencil factory. *Photo courtesy of Walker Powell and Tri-Lakes Daily News.*

In 1907, the steamer Liberty traveled from St. Louis to the Ozarks, going down the Mississippi and coming up the White River. *Photo courtesy of Pat Wood and Tri-Lakes Daily News.*

miles east of Branson). A vigilante group was formed to stop the lawlessness, and because they chose the desolate mountaintops (called balds) to hold their secret meetings, they became known as the Bald Knobbers.

In the beginning, the organization brought law and order to the region. However, after a time certain powerful and unscrupulous members began committing crimes themselves. Harold Bell Wright wrote in *The Shepherd of the Hills* that during the time of the Bald Knobbers "the law of the land was the law of rifle and rope."

To halt the continuous discord, a small number of residents formed their own vigilante band. They called themselves the "Anti-Bald Knobbers." In 1888, after the Bald Knobbers' violent leader, Nat Kinney, was killed at the hands of the Anti-Bald Knobbers, peace came to the area for the first time since the Civil War.

The Birth of a Town

In the 1870s a logging community began growing along the banks of the White River near Roark Creek. Reuben S. Branson opened a general store and post office near the activity, and in 1882 officially listed the new township as Branson.

After the St. Louis Iron Mountain and Southern Railway came to town in 1906, the fledgling community began to flourish. By 1912 Branson had a bank, a hardware store, a hotel, a school and a church. Farming and logging were the town's principal industries, but soon other entrepreneurs saw Branson's potential. Two of the largest factories in town were the Winch Spoke Company and the American Pencil Company.

Long before trout fishing was introduced, Ozark entrepreneur Jim Owen (standing on right with leg crossed) ran a popular fishing-guide service on Lake Taneycomo. Owen and his employees are pictured in this 1939 photo in front of another of his ventures, the Owen Theater. *Photo courtesy of James Haskett and Tri-Lakes Daily News.*

The Shepherd of the Hills

Not long after the turn of the 20th century, a backwoods preacher and writer named Harold Bell Wright camped on a mountaintop outside of town to write a novel. He titled his story *The Shepherd of the Hills*. After its publication in 1907, the tale of love, intrigue, and suspense set in the Ozark hills became a best seller.

The book's enormous popularity brought nationwide attention to the Ozarks. Soon scores of readers began visiting the area to see for themselves the countryside Wright had so beautifully described, and to meet the story's colorful characters. Although the novel was fiction, Wright had used various local citizens as models.

Lake Taneycomo

In 1911, the first dam to generate hydroelectric power on this section of the White River was constructed east of Branson, near Forsyth. Although officially titled the Ozark Beach Dam, it became known by locals as "Powersite Dam." The water that backed up above the dam became known as Lake Taneycomo (derived from <u>Taney</u> <u>Co</u>unty, <u>Mo</u>.). A resort town named Rockaway Beach, built along the banks of the new lake, quickly became a mecca for wealthy vacationers. *(Chapter Six will guide you on a car tour to Rockaway Beach, Forsyth, and Powersite Dam.)*

During the 1920s the Branson lakefront became a vacation hot spot. Wealthy visitors coming to Branson could spend their days boating, fishing and swimming. In the evening they would dance the night away. Jazz was the country's favorite music, and orchestra-equipped paddlewheels carried festive revelers from Branson to Rockaway Beach and back again.

The Savage White River

A constant threat to all the communities nestled in the

hollows along the banks of the White River was the river itself. During heavy rains the usually docile stream could become a devastating torrent, destroying the same roads and towns year after year. To combat the severe flooding, Congress in 1941 approved a four-dam flood control and hydroelectric power project.

Three of the dams were to be built in Arkansas and one in Missouri. Norfork Dam, constructed on the North Fork River near Mountain Home, Arkansas, was the first to be constructed. Bull Shoals Dam was completed in 1951, and Table Rock Dam began operation in 1959. When Beaver Dam (near Eureka Springs, Arkansas) was completed in 1964, the once mighty White River was finally controlled.

Trout Fishing Comes to Branson

The construction of Table Rock Dam added a new dimension to Branson—trout fishing. Due to the 48-degree water (you'll notice there are no swimmers in this lake) pouring into Lake Taneycomo from the bottom of Table Rock Lake, Taneycomo could no longer support its native warm-water fishery. The frigid water temperature did, however, provide the ideal environment for trout—a fish that thrives in cold water.

As the dam neared completion, the Army Corps of Engineers together with the Missouri Dept. of Conservation began raising trout at the Shepherd of the Hills Hatchery for later introduction into the future cold waters of Lake Taneycomo. (Although Taneycomo is technically a lake, because it has a dam at each end of its 22-mile length, it still maintains the look and feel of a river.) The Corps releases about 70,000 rainbows and browns into Lake Taneycomo each month, safeguarding its reputation as one of the best trout spots in the country.

The First Country Music Show

Something else took place in the 1950s that was to change

Branson's destiny. Performing in a 50-seat auditorium above the downtown city hall, the Mabe brothers (calling themselves The Baldknobbers) opened Branson's first music show. They presented a down-home country blend of music mixed with plenty of knee-slappin' comedy.

Country music wasn't really new to Branson. The sound of the fiddle, harmonica, dulcimer and mandolin had been heard at barn raisings and church gatherings since those first pioneers settled along the While River. But now, visitors coming to Branson for a glimpse of Ozark traditions and country living could also experience the country sound.

Silver Dollar City

In 1960 the Herschend family founded an old-time frontier town near Marvel Cave and gave it the name Silver Dollar City. Nationwide attention focused on Silver Dollar City when the producers of *The Beverly Hillbillies* filmed five segments of their then hit TV series there. The exposure spawned an interest in Branson and in handmade crafts that spread across the country. *To find out more about Silver Dollar City, see Chapter Four.*

Country Music Takes Center Stage

In 1967 another musical family, the Presleys, opened a theater featuring a trademark hillbilly character known as Herkimer. In the early '70s, the Foggy River Boys, the Plummer Family, and Bob Mabe built theaters along W. Mo. 76.

In 1981, after the movie *Urban Cowboy* became a hit, country music's popularity soared. Ten theaters opened in Branson within five years. Several of these theaters began featuring widely known entertainers as special guests. These performers liked what they saw in Branson. Not only was it a friendly and safe place to live, but they could now perform at one location without having to travel from city to city on concert tours.

In 1983 the first universally recognizable country star, Roy Clark, put his name permanently on a Branson marquee. In 1987, BoxCar Willie opened his theater, and in the next six years the music scene in Branson exploded. Entertainers opening theaters included Shoji Tabuchi, Cristy Lane, Mel Tillis, Mickey Gilley, Ray Stevens, Moe Bandy, Jim Stafford, Andy Williams, Willie Nelson, Jimmie Rodgers, the Osmond Brothers, Loretta Lynn, John Davidson and Wayne Newton. Some of these stars are no longer performing in Branson, but others, such as Tony Orlando and Bobby Vinton, have come to add their names to the growing list of performers who call Branson home.

Branson Becomes a Star

The catalyst for Branson's most recent growth came in 1991, after CBS' *Sixty Minutes* aired a segment on the "Branson Boom." Visitors that year came in such large numbers that it was difficult to find accommodations. Developers started building motels at breakneck speed, and more stars opened theaters. By 1998 Branson had more than 35 theaters, over 50,000 theater seats, and almost 7 million visitors yearly.

Shepherd

of the Hills

Homestead

**Ruth and Paul Henning
Conservation Area**

Homestead Tour

Inspiration Point

**Shepherd of the Hills
Outdoor Drama**

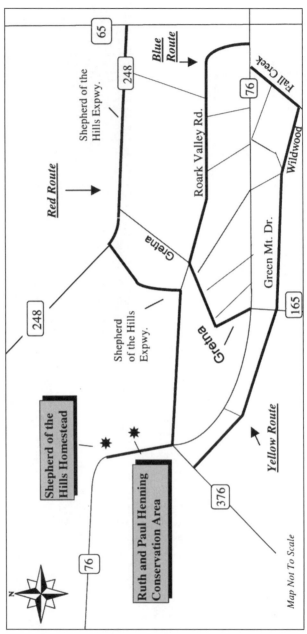

Shepherd of the Hills Homestead. *Use Time Saver Routes to avoid traffic on the Strip.*

Shepherd of the Hills Homestead

Telephone: (417) 334-4191 or (800) 653-6288
Web site: www.theshepherdofthehills.com

The wild Ozark countryside was like nothing he had ever seen. Hilltops presented compelling views of distant mountain ranges, tree-covered valleys and jagged hillsides carved from stone. Some of the terrain was crowded with giant oaks and blanketed with lush undergrowth. In other places, the land was barren and scattered with rocks and boulders, making the going slow and tedious.

It had stormed the last two days of his journey, and the steep grade leading to the river crossing was muddy and deeply rutted. When he finally reached the river, the traveler found that the rains had turned the usually gentle stream into a raging torrent, too dangerous to cross. A light shone on a distant hilltop, and the discouraged wanderer made his way toward it. J.K. Ross answered the knock at the door and welcomed the wet and weary stranger into his home.

The stranger in need was Harold Bell Wright, a preacher, artist, and writer from Kansas, traveling through Missouri on his way to Arkansas. J.K. Ross, his wife, Anna, and their son, Charley, soon became fast friends with the educated gentleman. Wright developed a passion for the Ozarks, and through the years he returned many times to visit the Ross farm.

In the summer of 1903 Wright arrived at the Ross cabin with a wagon packed with camping equipment. After setting up camp in a nearby cornfield, he began to write a story about a family like the Rosses, living in the Ozarks. He titled it *The Shepherd of the Hills.*

Harold Bell Wright. *Photo courtesy of Tri-Lakes Daily News.*

After publication in 1907, the romantic and suspenseful tale became the first novel in publishing history to sell over one million copies. The book's enormous popularity not only altered the lives of the kind family that aided Wright that dreadful night, it also changed the destiny of the entire Ozark region.

Why has the Shepherd of the Hills Homestead remained popular for almost a hundred years? Perhaps it's because the park is a living memorial to our country's heritage, reminding us all not only of the struggles and hardships our ancestors endured, but also of the enjoyment of life, love, and family that exists from generation to generation.

Today, at The Homestead, you can step back a hundred years and visit the Ross cabin and the site where Harold Bell Wright created his celebrated story. In the evening, you can sit under the stars and watch the classic tale come alive on stage.

A team of Clydesdales pulls a wagon near Old Matt's Cabin at the Shepherd of the Hills Homestead. *Photo courtesy of Shepherd of the Hills Homestead.*

What to See and Do

- **Inspiration Point**—ride the glass elevator to the top of a 230-foot observation tower for a thirty-five-mile view of the Ozarks.
- **The Shepherd of the Hills Outdoor Drama**—the play, presented nightly, features eighty actors, plus horses, wagons, gunfights, and a log cabin that is set ablaze during each performance.
- **Wagon and Horseback Rides**—take a ride in a wagon pulled by giant Clydesdales or wander the hills on horseback.
- **Harold Bell Wright Museum and Theater**—besides historical artifacts and manuscripts, there's a thirty-minute film about Wright and his accomplishments.
- **The Homestead Tour**—activities include a narrated tram ride to Old Matt's Cabin, Inspiration Point, and the outdoor amphitheater. The Harold Bell Wright Museum and wagon rides are also included in the Homestead Tour.

Hours

Inspiration Tower is open year-round. The rest of the park operates from May to late October, Monday through Saturday (except for a few weekdays in May and August). Call and check their schedule when you're in town. The park opens at 9 A.M.

Admission Price Ranges

The Complete Pass: adults $29.95; children (sixteen and

under) $14.95. Includes tour of Old Matt's Cabin, Inspiration Tower, Harold Bell Wright Museum, a *free* dinner, and the outdoors drama.

The VIP Complete Pass: adults $31.95; children $15.95. All the activities listed above *plus* VIP seating at the show (refreshments included).

Inspiration Tower: adults $5; children $2

Horseback Trail Rides: $12. Enjoy a forty-five-minute ride through the Ozark Mountains from Memorial Day to Labor Day. Children must be seven years old to ride. Pony rides for children six and under are $2.

Clydesdale Drawn Wagon Rides: adults $5; children $3.

Families can save money by purchasing a family pass. For $79.95 the entire family (children under sixteen) can enjoy all items listed under the Complete Pass option.

Ticket prices are subject to change at any time. Check their web site, www.theshepherdofthehills.com, for up-to-date prices.

Tips, Tactics & Timesavers!

- It's worthwhile to take the Homestead Tour before you see the play.
- A *free* buffet-style dinner is served before each show. You'll have a choice of fried chicken, barbequed brisket, corn on the cob, mashed potatoes and gravy, biscuit with honey butter and iced tea, lemonade, or coffee. Just be sure to head out early to avoid the crowd and get a seat indoors.
- Ozark nights cool down nicely, so you might want to take a long-sleeved shirt to the outdoor play. If the weather is really chilly, taking a blanket to wrap up in is a good idea.
- Directions for all day trips begin and end at the Missouri. 76 and U.S. 65 intersection. Travel tips are given about the Time Saver Routes.

How To Get There

The Shepherd of the Hills Homestead is located on **W. Missouri 76**, about 8 miles west of U.S. 65. Since this course is through the most congested section of the Strip, it's best to use one of the Time Saver Routes.

Travel Tips!

The Red Route bypasses all of the most heavily traveled areas on the Strip *(see the Red Route map in Chapter One)*. You can also use the Blue Route in combination with the Red Route. Follow Roark Valley Rd. (don't turn on Gretna) to the Shepherd of the Hills Expressway. Turn left and follow the Expressway to W. Missouri 76. Turn right to begin heading west. After passing the Country Tonite Theatre, you'll begin heading uphill.

Included on your day trip to Shepherd of the Hills Country is a stop at the **Ruth and Paul Henning Conservation Area,** featuring a spectacular scenic view and two hiking trails. The entrance to the Conservation Area is located on the right near the top of Dewey Bald Mountain (about 7/10 of a mile west of Shepherd of the Hills Expressway).

Ruth & Paul Henning Conservation Area

Paul Henning, the producer of *The Beverly Hillbillies,* donated this 1,534-acre tract of land to the state to assure the preservation of its natural beauty and wildlife. Much of the park's acreage contains steep, rock-strewn hillsides (glades) and stony knobs of rock devoid of vegetation, called "balds." Information in the following section will help you better understand the Ozarks' unique and varied geological characteristics.

Ozark Geology

The Ozark mountain range covers roughly 33,000 square miles in Missouri, Arkansas and Oklahoma. The region's highest point, at 2,250 feet, is Mt. Sherman in the Boston Mountains in Arkansas. Although the mountains are not impressive in height, age is another story. The oldest portions of the Ozark Mountains are about 500 million years of age—that's 300 million years older than the Rockies.

The following excerpt was written by Tom Aley, director of the Ozark Underground Laboratory, and taken from *In the Heart of Ozark Mountain Country.* The book, published by White Oak Press, is a popular, comprehensive history of the local area. Look for it in bookstores.

"The term 'Ozark Mountains' is somewhat of a misnomer. As an old saying goes: the Ozarks region does not have high mountains, just deep valleys. Though sometimes told as a joke, the statement is highly accurate: the region is a former plateau that has been dissected and eroded by countless streams, creating a land of valleys, rolling hills, and winding ridge tops.

"The visitor to the Ozarks may be struck by many unusual features in the landscape: matching bluffs on opposite sides of a valley, hillsides bestrewn with rocks, cedar- or grass-covered glades in the midst of an oak-hickory forest, and numerous

caves. To understand why the present landscape looks the way it does, we must first understand what shaped the land in the distant past.

"Millions of years ago, the Ozark region was covered by a shallow sea. Countless shelled animals died and left their remains on the sea floor. As these accumulated, they became compressed into rock, specifically limestone and dolomite. Mixed in with these rocks are a little bit of sandstone, some shale, and a lot of chert.

"The valleys have been formed by the action of streams cutting downward into the plateau which predated our present topography of hills and hollows. As the water cut its course down through the landscape, it commonly left bluffs on both sides of the water's course. Thus to this day in many places in the Ozarks, you can stand on a ridge and see other ridges in the distance at the same elevation with the same type of rock.

"The chert, much of which occurs as nodules or thin beds within the limestone and dolomite, is essentially insoluble. Then when limestone and dolomite, which are soluble in slightly acidic water, dissolve away, chert is left behind and accumulates. That is why most of the soils of the region are so rocky, at times causing entire hillsides to be fields of stone. Because thin soils do not hold much moisture and thus cannot support a hardwood forest, the vegetation of the glades is dominated by plants capable of tolerating drought-susceptible shallow soils: native grasses and Eastern red cedars.

"If the Ozark region were to be described geologically with one phrase, it might best be called 'The Land of Hollow Hills.' Beneath both the hills and the valleys lie extensive cave systems. Like the surface landscape, caves are formed because limestone and dolomite can be dissolved by water. The openings of caves originally form along fractures (called joints) and along the bedding planes, which separate adjacent layers of rock. These joints and bedding planes are slowly widened through time as water dissolves away more and more rock. As the valleys deepen, the caves are drained and the passages become open, allowing cave formations to begin growing.

"Cave country is characterized not only by caves, but also by springs, sinkholes, and disappearing streams. Caves and springs have long been thought of as features isolated and totally separate from the surface of the land where man normally spends his time. But it is important that we understand that the surface and subsurface are not separate worlds, but instead are part of the same system.

"In the Ozarks, we actually live on a sponge where the voids are capable of transporting contaminated water from one point to another. Contaminants allowed to sink into the ground may reappear in short order in a cave, well, or spring. During your time here, whether you are a resident or visitor, think before depositing anything on the ground that you would not want in a glass of your own drinking water."

A Bit of Ozark History

After the Civil War, a lawless vigilante group roamed this region of the Ozarks. Because they chose to hold their clandestine meetings on the barren mountaintops (so no one could sneak up on them undetected), they acquired the name "Bald Knobbers." Wright included the infamous Bald Knobbers in his story *The Shepherd of the Hills*, and you'll see them ride again during some of the outdoor drama's most exciting scenes.

Several sites immortalized in Wright's novel are located within the Ruth and Paul Henning Conservation Area. All of the following locations are known to be on this tract of land: Sammy Lane's Lookout, the Signal Tree, Little Pete's Cave, Dewey Bald Mountain and a portion of the "trail that is nobody knows how old."

Hiking Trails

If you would like to take a short hike, a paved trail leading to a 40-foot observation tower begins near the park's entrance. To find **Dewey Bald Trail**, follow the walkway past the restrooms and into the woods. You'll be heading up a fairly steep section of Dewey Bald Mountain, but the trail has several switchbacks to make for easier climbing. If you climb the tower, your effort will be rewarded with a breathtaking view of the hills and hollows surrounding Branson. It takes about 30 minutes to hike the half-mile trail.

A longer trail, called the **Boulder Glade Trail** (about 1.7 miles), begins at the observation deck. If you take the first loop back, the walk is about 1 mile. Both trails are exceptionally beautiful in the spring and fall.

From May to October, the **Missouri Department of Conservation**, (417) 334-3324, offers free guided nature walks on Tuesday, Thursday and Saturday. The group meets at 9 A.M. at the observation deck. This is an excellent chance to find out more about the Ozarks' rugged countryside and wildlife. It's not necessary to make reservations, but it's best to call to verify dates, as they are subject to change.

When ready to leave the park, turn right and follow W. Missouri 76 about one mile to the entrance to **Shepherd of the Hills Homestead.**

Turn right off Mo. 76 and right again to head toward the parking area. If there are no parking spots up front, continue driving through the tunnel (under the highway) to the main parking lot. A tram will take you back to the entrance.

Shepherd of the Hills Homestead

The **Lizzie McDaniel Ticket Office** is located in the row of buildings near the entrance. Along here you'll also find restaurants and gift shops. Among them is the **Precious**

Moments Animated Showcase and Gift Gallery, which features Samuel J. Butcher's Precious Moments figurines.

(For information about visiting the Precious Moments Chapel in Carthage, Missouri, see Chapter Eleven.)

The Homestead Tour

If you're going to take the tour, follow the walkway to the gate and make reservations for a seat on the next available tram. The guided tour lasts about one hour.

J.K. Ross (on the right) at his sawmill on Roark Creek. *Photo courtesy of Tri-Lakes Daily News.*

Old Matt's Cabin

The first point of interest on the tour is Old Matt's Cabin. This weathered-gray, century-old log home is where Harold Bell Wright sought refuge that rainy evening so long ago. It's called Old Matt's Cabin because Old Matt was the fictional name given J. K. Ross in Wright's novel. His wife was given the name Aunt Mollie, and his son became Young Matt. Local residents from nearby communities, including Levi Morrill (renamed Uncle Ike), the postmaster from the nearby town of Notch, were also used as models for the book's characters. Although the story was entirely fiction, many of the book's readers insisted on calling the Rosses and Morrill by their mythical names. So many visitors came to the region wanting to meet Old Matt, Aunt Mollie and Uncle Ike that over time, the Rosses and Morrill adopted the fictitious names as their own.

By 1906 the Rosses had moved away from the little cabin on the hill to operate a store and post office near Roark Creek. After *The Shepherd of the Hills* was published, a year later, tourists visiting the neglected homestead began pilfering bits and pieces of the Rosses' mill and cabin for souvenirs, causing it to deteriorate quickly.

A silent motion picture, filmed in 1919, renewed interest in the Homestead and a female entrepreneur, Pearl "Sparky" Spurlock, bought the uncared-for property to operate as a tourist attraction. Dressed in calico and smoking a corncob pipe, Sparky drove tourists up and down the rocky hillsides, passionately narrating the area's history.

Several other motion pictures about *The Shepherd of the Hills* have been released through the years. The most popular version, filmed in 1941, and starring John Wayne, is available (as the book is) in the gift shop.

The homestead's next owner, Lizzie McDaniel (the daughter of a wealthy Springfield banking family), was responsible for many of the cabin's present furnishings. After buying the rundown farm in the 1920s, Lizzie refurbished the dilapidated cabin and went about the countryside looking to buy back the belongings of the Ross family (by this time, both

Old Matt's Cabin. *Photo courtesy of Shepherd of the Hills Homestead.*

J. K. and his wife had passed away). To expand her business, Lizzie used part of the tiny cabin for a museum and tearoom.

During the tour of the cabin, your guide will give some historical highlights, and a group picture taken on the cabin's front steps will be available for purchase at the end of the tour.

Inspiration Point

"If thou art worn and hard beset,
with sorrows, that thou wouldst forget;
if thou wouldst read a lesson, that will keep
thy heart from fainting and thy soul from sleep,
go to the woods and hills! No tears.
Dim the sweet look that nature wears."

— *The Shepherd of the Hills*

It was on this hilltop, in 1903, where Harold Bell Wright set up a tent and began seeking inspiration for his novel. Wright's love of the Ozarks glowed brightly through his written words. He portrayed the hill folk as hardworking, generous people, and the countryside as beautiful as any place on earth. One of Wright's hill country characters, "Preachin' Bill," is quoted as saying, "When God looked upon th' work of his hands an' called hit good, he war sure a lookin' at this here Ozark country." Wright was able to paint such a lifelike picture of the area's charms that shortly after the book was published, sightseers began arriving by the thousands to meet the book's characters and see the Ozark countryside.

Inspiration Point is the highest point in southwest Missouri, and the second highest in the entire state. On a clear day you can see all the way to the Boston Mountains in Arkansas. Inside the tower, a glass elevator will carry you 230 feet up for a breathtaking 35-mile, 360-degree panoramic view of the Branson area. One flight down from the main level is an open-air observation deck with telescopes for close-up viewing.

The Country Church

The next stop will be at a century-old chapel. Originally built in Morgan, Missouri, in the 1901, the church was moved and reassembled on this site in 1989. Much of the building had to be rebuilt, but the ornate doors, windows, bell tower, pews, and pulpit are all original.

Old Mill Theater

Your next stop is the **Outdoor Amphitheater,** where the drama is presented each evening. At the amphitheater, you'll witness a milling demonstration, be entertained by a country music band, and visit the General Store.

In 1946, after the death of Lizzie McDaniel, Dr. Bruce Trimble and his wife, Mary, bought the homestead. It was Dr.

Trimble's vision to build an amphitheater for outdoor productions of Wright's novel. He died before he could see his dream fulfilled, but on August 6, 1959, Mary and her son Mark presented their first performance of the beloved story in the **Shepherd of the Hills Old Mill Theater.**

Local residents, most without any theatrical experience, became actors, and many went on to perform for years, with their children and grandchildren carrying on the tradition. The Homestead's present owner, Gary Snadon, portrayed one of the play's lead characters during the 1960s.

The entire set, from the stage to the cabin at the far end, is used during the two-hour evening production. In the first act, the stage is the setting for a country hoedown, complete with fiddlers and square dancers. Throughout the show, the vast open ground area is utilized for horses, sheep, wagons, gunfights, fistfights and a vintage automobile. During the dramatic scene where the Bald Knobbers set fire to the log cabin, flames leap as high as the treetops.

Story of the Shepherd of the Hills

Harold Bell Wright's novel is about a family struggling to survive in the Ozark hills during the late nineteenth century. One of the story's main characters is "Young Matt." Young Matt lives with his father, "Old Matt," and his mother (known by the hill folk as "Aunt Mollie") in a log cabin just west of Dewey Bald Mountain. Young Matt is in love with a beautiful girl called "Sammy Lane." Sammy, unaware that Young Matt is in love with her, has agreed to marry another suitor, "Ollie Stewart." "Wash Gibbs," a sinister member of the Bald Knobbers gang and an acquaintance of Sammy's father, "Jim," is also interested in Sammy.

An element of mystery is introduced when an educated, gentle stranger comes to the hills. He befriends Old Matt's grandson "Little Pete" and begins tending sheep in Mutton Hollow. He becomes known by local citizens as "the shepherd." The shepherd arouses suspicion, however, when he refuses to tell anyone where he came from or why he chose to reside in Mutton Hollow.

Do Young Matt and Sammy Lane end up together? Is Sammy Lane's father an outlaw? What secret is the stranger hiding from the folks at Mutton Hollow? The story weaves an entertaining tale of romance, mystery and suspense.

At the tour's end, the tram will head uphill (watch out for the moon shiners!), and return you to the entrance.

Christmas at the Homestead

The Homestead puts on a spectacular show during the holidays. From the first of November through the first week in January, the park presents "The Trail of Lights." First, there's the tower, decorated from top to toe with the beautiful lights and sounds of Christmas—don't miss making a trip up the tower for an awesome view of Branson at Christmastime. Then, there's the trail, lined with hundreds of animated holiday displays and viewed from the warmth of your own car. Santa will be there too! Admission prices (includes the tower) on Friday and Saturday are: adults $7; children $4. The rest of week the price for adults is $5 and children $3. *Hours and prices may change, so be sure to call for the current schedule.*

The Way Back

To get back to your starting point, you could follow W. Missouri 76 all the way to U.S. 65. Since this route would take you through the most congested areas of the Strip, however, it's best to use one of the Time Saver Routes.

Silver Dollar City

What to See and Do

How to Get There

Inside the Park

History of Silver Dollar City

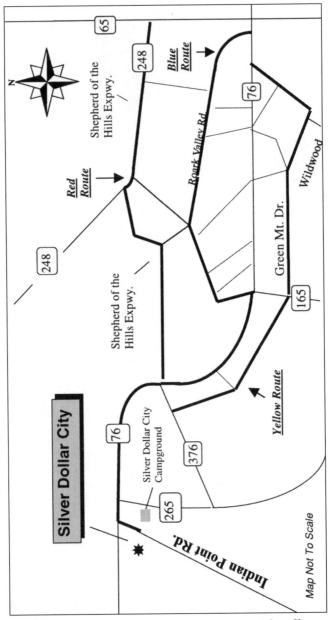

Silver Dollar City. *Use Timesaver Routes to avoid traffic on the Strip.*

Telephone: (417) 336-7100 or (800) 831-4FUN
Web site: www.silverdollarcity.com

A blanket of white mist cloaks the Ozark hills as the sun begins to warm the new day. Down in the hollow, songbirds warble soft wake-up calls to the cadence of buhrstones grinding the first load of grain at the old weathered mill. Echoing through the hills is the resonant sound of steel on iron as the overall-clad blacksmith compels hot metal to bend to his will.

The baker has been busy since dawn, and an irresistible aroma wafts from racks already lined with neat rows of fresh-baked loaves. Up on Main Street, stores are beginning to open. A bell jingles from the movement of a sturdy oak door, and calico ruffles brush clean-swept floorboards as a clerk scurries to put things right for the first customer of the day.

This isn't a scene from the 1890s; it's happening today at Silver Dollar City (SDC)—a picture-perfect, flower-filled frontier village, where the townsfolk will greet you with a "Howdy" just to make you feel welcome.

No trip to Branson would be complete without a visit to this theme park served up "country style." If you think you're too old—you're not! If you think it's just an amusement park with wild and crazy rides—it isn't! There's a good reason why SDC has been Branson's most talked about attraction for over 30 years—it's just great fun for everyone!

What to See and Do

- Enjoy musical entertainment from morning till night on nine separate stages.
- Tour Marvel Cave—the attraction that started it all.
- Stroll tree-shaded pathways lined with dozens of shops brimming with everything from crafts and country art to fine jewelry.
- Witness a feud between the Hatfield and McCoys that's been a-goin' on for over thirty years.
- See resident crafters create decorative and useful items the old-fashioned way—by hand.   Daily demonstrations include glass blowing, basket weaving, woodcarving, candy making and more.
- Dine at any of the park's dozen or so homestyle restaurants featuring SDC's made-from-scratch breads and desserts.
- Take an excursion on a vintage railroad, ride a roller coaster through a silver mine, raft down a white-capped river, and join in the fun on lots of other country theme rides.   The little ones will find a kid-size amusement park just for them.
- In the evening, you'll clap your hands and tap your toes at a two-hour country music review.

Over 100 resident craftsmen are featured daily at Silver Dollar City.

Tips, Tactics & Timesavers!

- Dress casually. There's a full day of entertainment ahead and your footwear and clothing should be your most comfortable.

- Take your camera. The entire park is a perfect backdrop for photos.

- Wear a watch so you can keep up with the show schedules.

- During the summer and fall, it's a good idea to arrive before the park officially opens. Otherwise, you may have a lengthy wait to get to the parking areas—traffic has been known to back up for miles. Having breakfast in the park is a good way to begin the day and miss the traffic. The all-you-can-eat country breakfast buffet starts at 8 A.M., April-October. If you do go later in the day, here's an alternate route that will bypass most of the traffic. Take one of the Time Saver Routes to W. Missouri 76 and Shepherd of the Hills Expressway. Head south on Missouri 376 (the continuation of the Expressway). Missouri 376 is a short scenic route that connects with Missouri 265. Turn right on 265 and follow it back to W. Missouri 76. Turn left on 76 and travel the short distance to Indian Point Road. Follow the signs to SDC.

- The park is usually less crowded on Wednesdays and Thursdays.

- If it rains on the day of your visit, ask about the bad-weather policy.

- Strollers, wheelchairs, electric carts, and lockers are all available for rent. There's also an ATM machine and a free "Package Pick Up" service (if you don't want to carry your packages around all day). Packages are delivered to the Guest Convenience Center near the entrance at 1 and 5 P.M.

- If visiting on Sunday, you can attend a non-denominational service held at 9:30 and 11 A.M. in the log church near the McHaffie Homestead.

- On a budget? Pack a lunch and return to your car for a tailgate picnic. Just be sure to have your hand stamped at the gate as you leave.

- If you plan to visit SDC more than once a year, consider buying a season pass. Even if you return only once, you'll save money.

- Another money saver is the "Combination Ticket." For a reduced rate, you can buy a single ticket that includes other SDC attractions such as White Water, Dixie Stampede, and the Showboat Branson Belle. Ask for details at the ticket booth.

- If you arrive after 3 P.M., the next day is free. If you have small children, or are a senior citizen, this option could work well for you. You can come after 3, visit one side of the park, have dinner and see the show at the amphitheater. The next day, you could come for breakfast and visit the rest of the park.

Hours

The park opens at 8 A.M. for the breakfast buffet and shopping. Shows and rides start at 9:30.

From early April to mid-May (the exact dates change yearly), the park is open Wednesday through Sunday. After Labor Day, it's closed on Mondays only until early November, when the Wednesday through Sunday schedule is resumed. In November and December the hours change to 1 P.M. (noon on Sat.) to 10 P.M.

During the last week of August and for a period of time in late October and early November, the park closes completely in order to prepare for the special seasons. Be sure to call if visiting during these times to check exact dates.

Admission Price Ranges

The admission range for adults is $36.05, children (4-11) are charged $24.35 and those 3 and under go free. Senior citizen (55+) price is $33.90. Admission is less during the Christmas season. Call for the exact price.

How To Get There

The shortest route from the **U.S. 65** and **Missouri 76** intersection is to head west on 76 for nine miles to **Indian Point Road.** After you reach Indian Point Road, just follow the signs to Silver Dollar City. This route, however, is through the most intense traffic in Branson and should be avoided if at all possible. Follow any of the Time Saver Routes to escape the congestion.

Travel Tips!

> The Red Route bypasses all of the most heavily
> traveled areas on the Strip *(see the Red Route map
> in Chapter One)*. You can also use the Blue Route
> in combination with the Red Route. Follow Roark
> Valley Rd. (don't turn on Gretna) to the Shepherd
> of the Hills Expressway. Turn left and follow the
> Expressway to W. Mo. 76. Turn right and travel
> about 4 miles to Indian Point Rd.

Inside the Park

A parking attendant will direct you to the closest available
lot, and a tram will take you to the main gate. The tram will
return you to the pick-up point when you're ready to leave—
no matter how late it is! Just be sure to remember the letter
assigned to your lot.

The map and the show schedule you'll receive when you
purchase your ticket are loaded with facts on finding your way
around, scheduled show times, rides and restaurants. Keep
them close at hand for easy reference. *Be sure to ask if they fail
to hand them to you.*

If you're interested in knowing about each ride before
hand (a few have height and size restrictions), pick up a
Rides Guidebook at the stroller booth near the entrance.

Here for Breakfast?

To find the breakfast buffet, go through the **Hospitality
House** and out the back door. From there, follow the street to

the right to **Molly's Mill Restaurant**. (Molly's Mill also serves buffets for lunch and dinner.) If you're looking for something lighter, the snack bar in the Hospitality House serves croissant and biscuit egg sandwiches, and **Eva and Delilah's Bakery** (at the entrance) offers luscious pastries, muffins and gourmet coffees.

The Hospitality House

The Hospitality House has a gift shop, snack bar, restrooms, an ATM machine, and the entrance to **Marvel Cave** (open to tourists since 1894). Features in the cave include icicle-like stalactites, stalagmites, dripstone formations and a fifty-foot waterfall. The guided tour, lasting about one hour, ends with a cable car ride back to the surface. (Be prepared for about seven hundred steps and one tight passageway.)

Hot Weather Tip!

If visiting on a warm day, you might want to wait and tour the cave later in the afternoon. That way you can use the cooler morning hours to see the outdoor areas of the park, and visit the "cool" cave during the heat of the day. *But, be sure to check the starting time of the last tour to make sure you don't miss it.*

Music Shows

Just beyond the Hospitality House is the town square. At the square's **Music Gazebo**, you can sit, listen to some country-style entertainment, and take a minute to look over the SDC map and show schedule.

Indoor and outdoor music shows (presented throughout the day) are a big part of the SDC experience. Music shows are presented on six outdoor stages and in three air-conditioned theaters; the latter include the **SDC Saloon** (lots of fun and laughs), **The Opera House** (a Broadway-style performance in a 1,000-seat auditorium) and the **Riverfront Playhouse** (performers vary). Be sure to arrange your schedule around these outstanding productions!

In the evening, the **Echo Hollow Amphitheater** presents a two-hour outdoor country music show beginning 30 minutes after the park closes. If it's too tiring to spend the entire day, you can leave any time and return before showtime.

What to See First

It's not easy to see and do everything SDC has to offer in just one day, but with this book and your SDC map, you'll be able to find your way around and not miss anything.

A good way to begin is by visiting the park's original attractions. From the Music Gazebo, cross Main Street (behind the gazebo) and follow the pathway next to Wings & Whispers downhill to **Grandfather's Mansion**. The kids will want to make more than one trip through this topsy-turvy funhouse where nothing's as it's supposed to be.

After visiting Grandfather's Mansion, continue walking downhill, turn left at the first road and follow it to **Huck Finn's Hideaway.** Entry to the tree house is by way of a gigantic tree trunk that leads to a suspended bridge and Huck's hideaway.

From the tree house, retrace you way back toward Grandfather's Mansion, and veer to the left, following the road to the **Silver Dollar Frisco Line Steam Train**. The twenty-minute ride will take you through the forest and give you a glimpse of what the rest of the park has to offer.

After exiting the train, retrace your way back the way you came, head uphill, and veer to the left when you reach Grandfather's Mansion again.

Be sure to wander through all the shops along here. In **Carrie's Candles** you can try your own hand at candle dipping, and next door at **Sullivan's Mill** the aroma of just-baked bread is sure to lure you inside for a sample and a grain-grinding demonstration. At the end of the street is the **Wilderness Road Blacksmith Shop,** where you can observe the blacksmith practicing his age-old craft.

When ready to leave the blacksmith shop, walk uphill, heading back to the square. Turn right on Main Street, and after checking out all the stores fronting Main, veer to the left (don't head downhill yet).

The first building you'll come to is **The Wilderness Church**. This weathered-gray log building originally served as a schoolhouse in the nearby community of Reeds Spring. After converting it into a chapel (the pulpit was made from a tree that was removed during construction of the park), SDC began holding Sunday services and country weddings. If you would like a picture-perfect country wedding, SDC can arrange a romantic 1880s-style ceremony, complete with a horse-drawn wagon and all the appropriate finery.

Next to the church is **McHaffie's Pioneer Homestead**. In 1960 this hundred-year-old, hand-hewn log home (once owned by the McHaffie family) was moved and reassembled on this site to save it from being destroyed by the backwaters of Bull Shoals Lake. Today, you'll find SDC's McHaffie clan busily going about their daily chores. Mrs. McHaffie is usually in her kitchen, while other family members are outdoors splitting wood, tending the garden or gathering eggs. And when their work is done, they'll all get to pickin' and singin' on the front porch.

This concludes the tour of the original park, before it expanded down the hill and into the hollow.

Exploring the Left Side of the Park

From the Homestead, follow the pathway downhill to

Silver Dollar Frisco Line Steam Train. *Photo courtesy of Silver Dollar City.*

begin your tour of the left side of the park. Two attractions not to miss are the shows at the **SDC Saloon** and **The Opera House**. Check your map for locations, and the show schedule for show times. You'll probably have to stand in line to see the saloon show, due to limited seating capacity, but it's hilariously funny and well worth the wait. There's plenty of room in the Opera House, however, so you can browse through the nearby craft village and easily find a seat just before show time, unless the park is really packed.

Rides on this side of the park include: **The Fire-in-the-Hole** (a small roller coaster will take you through a blazing mining town), the **American Plunge** (a water ride ending in a splashdown that may get you wet), **BuzzSaw Falls** (a wet-dry roller coaster with tops speeds of fifty miles an hour), and **Wildfire**. Wildfire, SDC's newest and fastest high-tech roller coaster, offers a vertical drop of fifteen stories and speeds up to sixty-six miles an hour.

One of the many shops along here is **The Book and Print Shop**. Here you can get your name printed on a wanted poster, or have a special edition of the SDC newspaper printed with any headline you choose. At the **Tintype Photo Shop**, located next door, they'll take your picture dressed in country garb and turn it into a tintype print—an old-fashioned souvenir that's sure to become a family heirloom.

If you have small children, you won't want to miss **Tom Sawyer's Landing**. To find it, follow the road in front of the SDC Saloon. This area features **Becky's Carousel**, **Tom's Skychase Balloons**, the **Runaway Ore Cart** (a roller coaster), the **Critter Corral** (a petting zoo), and lots of secret places for kids to explore.

Restaurants near Tom Sawyer's Landing include: **Lumbercamp Restaurant** (grilled hamburgers and chicken sandwiches); **Aunt Polly's** (red beans and rice with sausage and chicken and noodles); and the **Riverside Rib House** (barbecued ribs, pork and chicken).

Exploring the Right Side of the Park

Two popular water rides on this side of the park are **The Lost River of the Ozarks** (whitewater rafting) and the **Wilderness Water Boggan**. Both are guaranteed to get you wet so you might want to watch from the sidelines to see what you're getting into.

Near the rafting ride are **Geyser Gulch** and **Splash Harbor**. Heralded as the world's largest tree house, Geyser Gulch, a multimillion-dollar playground in the sky, consists of a series of towers connected by rope crawls, swinging bridges, and tunnels. Throughout the tree house, children (and their parents and grandparents) can explore more than one hundred interactive and fun things to do. There are moving targets, windmills, whirligigs, sirens, slides, telescopes, and gadgets and gizmos that spew water, shoot foam balls, and make wacky sounds. All the action causes the pressure to build until a giant geyser erupts. Adjacent to Geyser Gulch the **S.S. Tadpole**, anchored in Splash Harbor, offers squirt gun fun for kids of all ages. You will get dripping wet at both these attractions.

The Dockside Theatre, **Boatworks Theatre**, and the **Riverfront Playhouse** (the Playhouse is air-conditioned) are all located at the lower end before starting up the hill.

Just after starting uphill, look for **Hillcreek Pottery,** where you can watch the master potter at the wheel, creating the hand-thrown stoneware sold in the shop. Further up the hill is the entrance to **Echo Hollow Amphitheater,** where the evening music show is performed. The two-hour country show is as entertaining as some on the strip—and you've already paid for it. If you're going to leave the park and return before show time, check the exact starting time and don't forget to have your hand stamped at the gate as you leave. You can usually get a parking space in lots A & B (the ones closer to the entrance) when you return. Another barbecue restaurant, **Poke Salad Mary's**, is near the amphitheater.

Just past Echo Hollow is a ride called **Shootout in the Flooded Mine** (good for any age from 2 to 92). For the more daring, a little further on is **Thunderation**, a roller coaster designed to give its riders the thrill of riding a speeding runaway train through an abandoned mine. It travels 3,000 feet in 2 minutes, 10 seconds and has a top speed of 48 mph.

Two more craft shops to browse are **Mountain Woodcarvers** and **Hazel's Blown Glass Factory**. The art of woodcarving thrives today, due in part to a revival that began right here in the Ozarks during the 1970s. If you're interested in woodcarving as a hobby, the resident craftsman will give you a demonstration to get you going.

The Way Out

After you reach the top of the hill, you'll be back at the square. If you're ready to leave the park, follow the pathway to the left, go through the Hospitality House, walk past the bakery and enter the **Ozark Marketplace**. At the back of the huge shop (crammed with all kinds of last-minute tempting stuff) is the exit ramp leading to the tram pick-up area. If you're leaving after the show at Echo Hollow, you'll exit where you entered in the morning.

SDC's Fabulous Festivals

World-Fest

In early spring, SDC welcomes more than five hundred performers from around the globe to America's largest international festival. Clowns from Russia, acrobats from

Japan, flag throwers from Italy, and dancers from such countries as Thailand and Japan will entertain visitors. And, you'll find exotic dishes such as Jamaican Ribs, Tandoori Chicken, Seafood Paella, and Wiener Schnitzel.

The Great American Music Festival

In late spring, nearly one thousand performers participate in this popular festival. In addition to the regularly scheduled music shows, various other shows take place all around the park. You'll hear country, Cajun, Dixieland, gospel, barbershop harmony, swing, jazz, bluegrass, and more.

National Kids' Fest

In the summer, there's even more good old-fashioned family fun at SDC. Just a few of the more than one hundred activities designed for kids are: sand art, pottery making, tie-dye, henna painting, scrapbook art, pie-eating contests, juggling, and face painting.

Festival of American Craftsmenship

From early September to the end of October, SDC gears up to celebrate the changing of the seasons. More than seventy-five of the nation's top award-winning artisans come to join the fun. The cool, crisp air, mixed with the scent of fresh-brewed coffee, wood-smoked meats, and just-picked apples, will exhilarate the taste buds and lift the spirit. Many tourists rate autumn as their favorite time of year to visit Silver Dollar City. (Most rides are open, as weather permits.) The park is closed on Mondays during this time.

Founder Mary Herschend and son Peter standing in front of the SDC General Store. *Photo courtesy of SDC.*

Old Time Country Christmas

From early November to the end of December, the village becomes a fairyland of twinkling lights and fanciful memories. Besides great holiday shopping, the park's featured attractions include: a living Nativity presented in theater-in-the-round, a sing-along train ride (the only ride open), and music shows featuring all the holiday classics. The park is open Wednesdays through Sundays during the holiday season.

The History of SDC

Silver Dollar City is here because Marvel Cave is here. The cavern was discovered, as legend has it, by an Indian hunting party. One day while looking for game on this ridge top, one of the tribe's braves suddenly vanished. While inspecting the area where he had disappeared, the Indians found the cave's entrance. They also discovered that the first step ended in a 200-foot drop straight down, which led them to name the cave "The Devil's Den."

During the 1860s a mining company began searching the cavern for lead ore. They didn't find any lead, but because they thought they had found a wall of solid marble, they named the underground passage "Marble Cave." Years later, another mining company found that the wall was really made of limestone.

In 1889 William Lynch bought the cave for $10,000 with the idea of operating it as a tourist attraction. He and his two daughters, Genevieve and Miriam, opened the cave for a time in 1894 and again in 1900 (it has remained open ever since).

Only the adventurous explored the cavern in those early days. Visitors determined to see the cave had to descend a ladder into total darkness guided only by candlelight. They had to climb up the same ladder to exit the cave. After their father's death in 1927, the two sisters changed the name to "Marvel Cave" and continued to run the business until the late 1940s.

Hugo and Mary Herschend, from Chicago, secured a 99-year lease from the Lynch sisters in 1949. Although access to the cavern had been improved, exiting the cave was still strenuous, and it was Hugo's plan to build a railroad to carry visitors back to the surface. He died before his dream could become a reality, but Mary and her two sons, Peter and Jack, proceeded with his design. In 1958, after a 218-foot tunnel was blasted through solid rock to make way for the tracks, the railroad was completed, and business jumped 40 percent.

To encourage more people to visit their attraction, Mary and her sons set about rebuilding the old mining town that once stood near the cave's entrance. Mary demanded that every aspect of each building be as authentic as possible. She also saw to it that the surrounding woodland remained as undisturbed as possible by insisting that only those trees directly in the path of streets or buildings be removed. Thanks to Mary's foresight, SDC duplicates—in precise detail—a century-old village nestled in a pristine Ozark forest.

The Herschends named their new "old" town Silver Dollar City, and in 1960 the park opened with a blacksmith shop, a general store, an ice cream parlor, the Wilderness Church, McHaffie's Homestead and a stagecoach ride. For a short time, real silver dollars were given as change. To provide additional entertainment for their visitors, Jack and Peter reenacted a mock gunfight between two feuding hill folk families, the Hatfields and the McCoys. Store clerks and cave guides left their posts every hour to participate in the rough and rowdy show.

Sullivan's Mill and the Frisco Silver Dollar City Line were added in 1962. Because the engine had to stop for a short time to build up a head of steam, a just-for-fun train robbery was added. Today, the members of the Alf Bolin Gang (a local band of outlaws during the Civil War) are still trying to rob the Frisco.

In 1963 Arkansas woodcarver Peter Engler opened a shop and began giving in-house demonstrations. Tourists loved his handmade country art, and soon other crafters opened shops in the park. That fall an autumn craft festival brought 500,000 visitors and Branson's first traffic jam.

SDC became the backdrop for five segments of *The Beverly Hillbillies* in 1969. The popular TV show was in its heyday, and the national exposure caused gate receipts to soar. During the next 25 years, amusement-park rides and a variety of music shows were added to enhance the park's appeal.

Although Mary Herschend is no longer alive, her two sons, Jack and Peter, still own the park. Through their hard work and dedication, SDC has remained one of the most entertaining family-oriented attractions in Missouri.

Several segments of *The Beverly Hillbillies* series were filmed during the '60s at SDC when the Clampett family came to the Ozarks looking for a husband for Ellie May. *Photo courtesy of SDC.*

The Way Back

Follow **Indian Point Road** back to **W. Missouri 76** and turn right. You could follow 76 all the way back to U.S. 65, but it's better to use any one of the Time Saver Routes.

Author's Note

I visited SDC for the first time as a teenager with my parents over 30 years ago. I returned later with my new husband and years after that with my three small children. As mementoes, I have a tintype photo of my children (now grown), a hand-carved hillbilly figure and a handmade clay vase. All have been a part of my home's decor no matter where I have lived. In 1994 the park's candle shop designed a unity candle in colors to match those chosen for my eldest son's wedding. SDC really does create lasting memories, and I know you'll take some home with you!

Branson's Free Attractions

College of the Ozarks

Table Rock State Park

Table Rock Dam

Shepherd of the Hills
Fish Hatchery

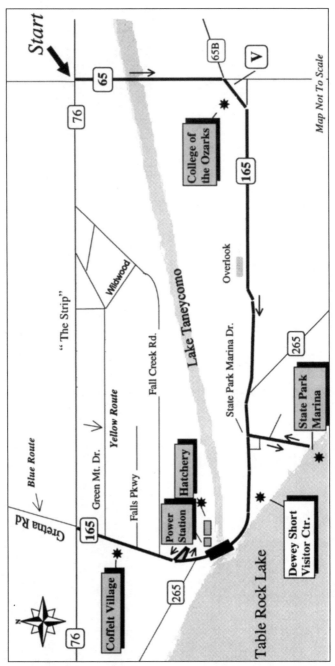

Branson's Free Attractions. *Approximate round-trip mileage: 20.*

The back roads of Branson will delight you with some of the most beautiful scenery you'll find anywhere in the Ozarks. One of these scenic byways is **Missouri 165**. Taking off U.S. 65 south of Branson, 165 heads west and then circles north to connect with Missouri 76 near the west end of the Strip.

Today's car tour of Missouri 165 is a great family outing; there are lots of fun things for kids to do, little time is spent in the car, and there are no admission charges to any of the attractions. Included in today's trip are suggestions of where you might like to have breakfast and lunch.

What to See and Do

- **College of the Ozarks**—150,000 visitors come each year to dine at the college restaurant, visit the working gristmill and enjoy the pretty campus.
- **Table Rock State Park**—here you can feed some hungry fish, learn about Ozark wildlife at the Dewey Short Visitor Center, and take a nature hike along Table Rock Lake.
- **Shepherd of the Hills Fish Hatchery**—the hatchery's visitor center features a film and wildlife exhibits.
- **Table Rock Dam**—just viewing the mammoth dam will take your breath away. For a small charge, you can take a guided tour.
- **Coffelt Country Crossroads Shopping Village**— a country-style village filled with flea markets and craft shops.

Tips, Tactics & Timesavers!

- It's best to take this tour Monday through Friday, when all the attractions are open.
- If you have any stale bread or crackers, take them along to feed the fish at Table Rock State Park. There's a fish-food vending machine, but the more you have, the more fun it is.
- Directions for all the tours throughout the book will begin and end at the Missouri 76 and U.S. 65 intersection.

How To Get There

Our suggestion for breakfast is the **Rose O'Neill Friendship House Restaurant** (417-334-6411 ext. 3341) at the College of the Ozarks. They are open for breakfast at 7 A.M. *Price Range: Low to Moderate.*

Even if you're not having breakfast at the Friendship House, stop at the restaurant and pick up a self-guided tour map of the campus. In the restaurant's gift shop, you'll find student-made crafts, jellies, baked goods and souvenirs.

To reach the **College of the Ozarks** from the **U.S. 65** and **Missouri 76** intersection, take U.S. 65 south for 2 miles to the stoplight at **State Road V**. Turn right and head west for a little more than half a mile. The restaurant is on the right near the entrance to the college.

This hometown college has seen lots of changes since it was founded as The School of the Ozarks in 1906. It became a junior college in 1956, a four-year liberal arts college in 1965, and was officially renamed College of the Ozarks in 1990. Unchanged, however, is the principle on which the college was founded. The aim of the school's founding fathers was "to provide a Christian education, especially for those found worthy, but who are without sufficient means to procure such training."

Appropriately called "Hard Work U," the school requires each student to work at a campus job to offset part of the cost of his or her education. Private endowments and gifts cover the balance. You'll encounter these working students throughout your visit—at the restaurant, mill, and fruitcake kitchen.

Your first stop on campus is **Edwards Mill** (Building 22 on the campus map). To reach the mill, enter through the gate at the main entrance, drive to the bottom of the hill, and turn right on Opportunity Ave. Travel one block and turn right again on Vocational Way.

Edwards Mill

Telephone: (417) 334-6411; Hours: Monday through Saturday, 9 A.M. to 4:30 P.M.; Season: Open year-round except for the last half of December and all of January

"What the club is to the city man, and the general store or post office to the citizens of the country village, the mill is to the native of the backwoods.

"Made to saw the little rough lumber he needs in his primitive building, or to grind his corn into the rough meal that is his staff of life, the mill does more for the settler than this; it brings together

the scattered population, it's the news center, the heart of the social life, and the hub of the industrial wheel."

—*The Shepherd of the Hills*

These words, written by Harold Bell Wright, illustrate how important the gristmill was to early life in the Ozarks. Edwards Mill preserves the disappearing memory of a once vital industry.

The college assembled the authentic-looking mill in 1972 with the support of Hubert C. Edwards, chairman of Dixie Portland Flour Mills. Much of the mill's weathered gray lumber and grinding machinery came from other non-working Missouri mills. The iron hubs in the water wheel came from an 80-year-old mill in Jackson, Missouri, and the mill's heavy timbers (between 80 and 100 years old) were brought from Carthage, Missouri. Power comes from a 12-foot wheel turned by runoff water from nearby Lake Honor.

Edwards Mill at the College of the Ozarks. *Photo courtesy of College of the Ozarks.*

The college uses the mill as a hands-on educational tool, a tourist attraction and a means of support. After students grind the whole grains, they blend them into various mixes and package them to sell. Available for purchase are flour and coarse-ground cornmeal (perfect for baking country-style cornbread), and a variety of mixes used for making pancakes, waffles, biscuits, muffins and funnel cakes. For a hearty and healthy treat, try the whole-wheat muffin mix.

Other old-time crafts practiced at the mill are weaving and basket making. Upstairs in the studio, students are busy weaving rugs, blankets, shawls and other items on hand-operated looms. All items are available for purchase, and all profits are used to support the college.

Fruitcake and Jelly Kitchen

Your next stop on campus is the **Fruitcake and Jelly Kitchen** (417) 334-6411 ext. 3395. After leaving the mill, travel back down the hill to **Opportunity Ave.**, cross the street, staying on **Vocational Way**, and go one block farther to Bldg. #16 (the stone building on your left just before the gate). The entrance is in the back of the building near the parking area.

The college has been baking its irresistible fruitcakes since 1934. In the kitchen, you'll be welcomed with a free sample and given a tour of the bakery, where students are busy mixing, baking, cooling, wrapping and labeling cakes that are available for purchase year-round. Student workers, along with a supervisor, bake more than 40,000 fruitcakes annually. (If the free sample isn't enough, the $1 cupcake is a perfect individual-sized treat.)

Also made in the kitchen are fresh fruit jams, jellies, preserves and apple butter—all make great gift items any time of year. You can have your order shipped anywhere within the continental U.S.

 # Williams Memorial Chapel

Your next stop is the **Williams Memorial Chapel** and **Point Lookout**. Turn right after exiting the kitchen parking area and retrace your way back to **Opportunity Ave.** Turn left and then left again on **Spiritual St.** Travel one block and park in the lot in back of the church (Bldg. #26). There's a wonderful photo spot near the chapel, so be sure to take your camera with you when leaving the car.

Built mainly by students in 1956, the massive gray stone church features neo-Gothic architecture, an 80-foot-high vaulted ceiling, and exquisite stained-glass windows. Attached to the chapel is Hyer Bell Tower, where orchestral bells chime at noon and 6 P.M. Sunday services, beginning at 11 A.M., are open to the public.

For one of Branson's best scenic views, follow the walk at the base of the church steps to **Point Lookout**. The body of water below, snaking its way through the tree-covered hills, is Lake Taneycomo. The white buildings you see in the distance are the Grand Palace Theatre and the Radisson Inn on the Strip.

Not included on today's tour because of time limits is the **Ralph Foster Museum** (to the right of the church if you're facing Point Lookout). The huge gallery, (the size of the building is deceiving) covering three levels, is filled with Ozark memorabilia of every type and description. You should allow at least an hour and a half to tour it. There is a nominal admission charge for adults, but children high school age and under go free. If you're an antique or history buff, or just want to learn more about the Ozarks, be sure to return when you have the time.

Star Schoolhouse

The last point of interest on campus is the **Star Schoolhouse** (Bldg. #30), to the right of the museum. You can walk to the schoolhouse from the chapel. Originally built in Barry County, Missouri, in 1863, the pretty, whitewashed one-room school is a nostalgic reminder of our country's early days. Everything in the school is original, including the worn wooden desks and the black potbellied stove.

This concludes your visit to the college, and you're now on your way to **Table Rock State Park** to feed the fish. Retrace your way back to the campus entrance (Academic Ave. takes you out) and **State Road V**. Turn right and travel one mile to where V intersects with **Missouri 165**. Turn right and begin heading west. The picturesque drive along Missouri 165 presents a scenic glimpse of Ozark Mountain Country's diverse ecosystem. At times the rugged hillsides may be covered with thick forests, while at other times the slopes are almost barren and strewn with rocks. A more in-depth look at the Ozarks' unique geology is given in Chapter Three *(see the Index for the Ruth and Paul Henning Conservation Area)*.

Be sure to stop at the **Scenic Overlook** for a majestic view of Table Rock Dam and Lake Taneycomo. The upscale subdivision on the far side of the lake is Pointe Royale, a gated community where several of Branson's top performers reside.

When ready to leave the overlook, continue traveling northwest on 165. It's about 2 miles from the overlook to the **Table Rock State Park Marina**. (Along the way, Missouri 265 will join 165, and the route will be marked as both.) The entrance to the park is on the left, and you'll have to look closely for a fairly small brown sign stating **State Park**

Marina. Turn left and follow **State Park Marina Drive** about half a mile down the hill to the lake and parking area.

Table Rock State Park

Table Rock State Park, encompassing 356 acres, is an outdoor lover's paradise. Recreational opportunities include camping, boating, fishing and hiking. For more information about the park, follow the signs to the park office or ask at the marina.

State Park Marina

The full-service marina (Telephone: (417) 334-3069) offers boat rentals (including jet skis and paddleboats), and sailing, parasailing, and scuba diving lessons.

To find the fish, follow the walkway onto the main dock and walk around to the far side of the store building. The first boat slip is always left open for the carp. The size of these fish may make you want to do some serious fishing, but not here; these fish are pets! (The fish-food vending machine is at the boat slip.)

Carp are prolific and breed rapidly. They prefer warm waters, especially shallow, mud-bottomed lakes. In the winter months (November-March) the carp stop feeding and stay near the bottom, so you won't find them at the dock.

When you're ready to leave the marina, retrace your way back to 165/265, and turn left. The entrance to the **Dewey Short Visitor Center** is a short distance past the entrance to the Showboat Branson Belle.

Dewey Short Visitors Center

Telephone: (417) 334-4104; Hours: 7 days a week, 9 A.M. to 5 P.M.; Season: Varies according to availability of funds

Dewey Short grew up in Galena, Missouri, a small town northwest of Branson. During his 24 years as a U.S. Representative, Short's speaking abilities and down-home honesty earned him the title of the "Orator of the Ozarks." One of his most notable accomplishments was Table Rock Dam; he worked for more than twenty years to attain approval for the project.

Take time to wander through the **Four Seasons Exhibit,** where you can learn about the Ozarks' year-round wildlife activity. The area's rugged oak and hickory forests teem with squirrels, opossums, bobcats, cottontail rabbits, skunks, raccoons, and an abundance of white-tailed deer.

If you look out the picture windows at the back, you're likely to spot one of the region's jewel-tinged hummingbirds. The outdoor feeders are usually busy with more than one of these pint-size creatures. With wings that can beat up to 79 times per second, the tiny, acrobatic hummingbird can hover almost stationary before darting up, backwards (the only bird capable of this maneuver) or sideways—all in the blink of an eye.

Some of the region's larger birds are turkeys, ducks, woodcocks, grouse, owls, geese, vultures, doves, herons and loons. In the winter the bald eagle comes to Missouri, and avid bird watchers search the skies for just one magnificent glimpse. Missouri has the largest wintering population of bald eagles in the Midwest.

While in the visitor center, don't miss the film **The Taming of La Riviere Blanche** (the White River). The documentary-style film illustrates the building of Table Rock Dam, and is an excellent prelude to the tour of the dam. The 20-minute film can be shown at any time—just ask one of the staff.

If you would like to take a nature walk along the shoreline, ask at the desk for a copy of the **Nature Trail Guide**. To reach the trailhead, exit through the back door of the visitor center and follow the walkway towards the woods. The short scenic hike is a great way to give the kids some exercise, but be sure to keep them on the path, as poison ivy

Table Rock Lake marinas can provide everything needed to put you into this peaceful scene. *Photo courtesy of Branson/Lakes Area Chamber of Commerce.*

grows everywhere in the Ozarks. Remember the old saying, "Leaves of three, leave them be."

The level, wooded trail is an easy hike, but if you choose not to walk the entire route, check the trail guide for a shortcut to take you back. At the far end of the trail (near loop #4) there's a road that heads down to the water. If you wait a few minutes you're likely to see one of the ducks (amphibious vehicles) from Branson come down this road and "splash down" into the lake. Don't be tempted to follow the road back, though; return to the trail and follow it back to the visitor center.

When ready to leave the Dewey Short Visitor Center and head to the **Shepherd of the Hills Fish Hatchery**, turn left on **165/265** and travel across the dam.

Table Rock Lake

Table Rock Lake's 857-mile shoreline provides abundant recreational opportunities. Bass fishing is the premier activity, but fishing is also good for crappie, walleye and catfish. Another popular sport is scuba diving. The lake has a number of submerged bridges and old homesteads that make it particularly interesting to scuba divers.

According to the Department of Natural Resources, the lake received its name from a rock shelf that stands high above the White River about a mile downstream from the existing dam site. The U.S. Army Corps of Engineers originally planned to build the dam at the site, but tests showed that the present location would be better suited geologically. However, the name Table Rock remained.

After crossing the dam, the road will begin circling to the right. Continue traveling on 165 (turning right at the Junction Route 76 stoplight) downhill to the entrance to the fish hatchery. There are no signs but the road (on the right at the very bottom of the hill) has guardrails on both sides, making it easy to spot. After traveling one block, you'll be at **Hatchery Road** and the entrance to the visitor center parking lot. But first, to get a good look at the dam and take a photo or two, turn right on Hatchery Rd. and follow it as it circles to the lakefront.

Table Rock Dam

Overwhelming, monumental and awesome are some of the adjectives you could use to describe Table Rock Dam. The massive dam, rising 252 feet above the riverbed, contains 1.23 million cubic yards of concrete and measures 6,423 feet in length. There are 10 floodgates at the top, and when these gates are opened the dam is an even more impressive sight. Unfortunately, this can cause severe flooding and damage to areas below the dam. It has been necessary to open all 10 gates fewer than two dozen times since the dam was completed in 1958. When ready to leave the dam, follow the road back to the visitor center.

The Shepherd of the Hills Fish Hatchery

Telephone: (417) 334-4865; Hours: 7 days a week, 9 A.M. to 5 P.M.; Season: Year-round

After completion of the dam, cold—48-degree—water from the bottom of the new Table Rock Lake began pouring into Lake Taneycomo. The frigid water temperature destroyed Taneycomo's native warm-water fishery (bass, perch and catfish). To preserve Taneycomo's reputation as a superior fishing lake, the Missouri Dept. of Conservation set about raising and releasing trout, a fish that thrives in cold water. The project has been so successful that to keep up with the demand, more than 70,000 rainbows and browns are released into the lake each month.

The Visitor Center

Featured here are nature exhibits, aquariums, and a video titled **White River Rainbows**. The 10-minute show depicts trout production from the fertilization of the egg to maturity— just ask one of the staff and they'll be glad to start it for you. *Be sure to take the time to see it.*

Outside at the hatchery, raceways teem with trout of various sizes. Each fish must be 10 inches long before it can be released into area streams, and it takes between 12 and 18 months for trout to grow to that length. Fish-food vending machines are near the main building.

Angler fishing below Table Rock Dam. *Photo courtesy of Missouri Dept. of Conservation.*

Children will enjoy visiting the hatchery building, where they can see tiny trout in all stages of development. Guided tours are given from 10 A.M. to 2 P.M. Monday through Friday, from Memorial Day to Labor Day.

Hiking Trails

There are four hiking trails on the hatchery grounds, and trail maps are available in the visitor center. One of the park's prettiest pathways is **The White River Corridor Trail**—a great hike any time of year. The shady 8/10 of a mile trail parallels Lake Taneycomo, and the lake's cool breezes will keep you comfortable even in the hottest weather.

The trail begins just below the **#7 Rearing Pond** (see the map you picked up at the visitor center). To get to the trailhead, turn right as you leave the parking area of the visitor center, and immediately turn right again at the first driveway. Travel down to the lake, turn left onto the graveled road, and follow it to the parking area in front of the pavilion. The trailhead begins at the end of the concrete sidewalk.

Trout Fishing

Trout anglers are especially fond of this upper section of Taneycomo. Clad in chest-high waders and armed with rods, reels and tiny fishing lures, they fish 24 hours a day in hopes of landing a lunker rainbow or brown. About the only thing that can interrupt their conscientious activity is the sound of the siren. The signal, emanating from the dam, is a warning that it's time to head for higher ground. The dam's engineers activate the alarm when they are about to put one or more generators "on line." This action will cause water to be released from the bottom of Table Rock Lake into Lake Taneycomo, raising the water level as much as 10 feet in 30 minutes. Posted signs caution anglers never to ignore the warning.

During the tour of the dam, you'll learn what "on line"

means and why the action causes Taneycomo's water level to rise so dramatically.

If you want to tour the dam (there is a small charge), retrace your way to Hatchery Road, turn left and follow the road to, and through, the open gates. The power distribution station is a short way down on the left.

> If you would rather eat lunch first and visit the dam later, it's not far (about three miles) to several restaurants. It wouldn't be much out of the way to have lunch and return to the dam later for the tour. The last tour begins at 4 P.M.

Powerhouse Tour

Season: Open daily, 9 A.M. to 5 P.M. (last tour leaves at 4) April 1 to October 31; Admission Range: $3 adults, children 5 and under go free

Just how does the dam produce electricity? When Table Rock Dam was constructed, four penstocks (a penstock is a sluice or shaft used for controlling the flow of water) were built 145 feet below what was to be the surface of Table Rock Lake. Each 18-foot-diameter penstock, beginning on the Table Rock side, slants at a downward angle and ends at a turbine. A shaft is located above the turbine, and above the shaft sits a generator.

During hydroelectric generation, water drawn from the depths of Table Rock flows down the penstock to the turbine, causing it to spin. (The flow of water used to turn the turbine is then released into Lake Taneycomo.) The spinning turbine rotates the shaft, which in turn spins the generator. The spinning generator produces fifty thousand kilowatts of electricity, which is routed from the powerhouse to the transformers. The onset of this process is known as putting a generator "on line."

The thirty-five minute, half-mile tour takes you deep inside the dam, where the generators are housed (if you're at all claustrophobic, you might want to wait in the lobby for the rest of the family). The tour includes 167 steps, but it's slow-paced and not strenuous. Tours are given every hour except at noon.

When ready to leave the dam and head to the restaurant, follow **Hatchery Road** (past the visitor center) to **Missouri 165**. Turn right and head north for about 2 miles.

Our suggestion for lunch is **The Bar B Q and Burger Shop**, on the left just past the Fall Creek Steak House (look for the giant bull) and the Fall Creek Inn. A favorite of locals, the restaurant (it's bigger on the inside than it looks) features burgers and delicious barbequed beef and pork sandwiches. Hours: Monday-Saturday, 11 A.M. to 3 P.M. *Price range: Low*

Another excellent choice for lunch is **Shorty Small's Great American Restaurant** (downhill on the other side of Falls Parkway). Shorty Small's features fall-off-the-bone barbecue ribs, but also has chicken-fried steak, burgers, nachos, salads, and more. *Price Range: Low to Moderate.*

When you're ready to continue, follow 165 up the hill for a few blocks and look on the left for the **Coffelt Country Crossroads Shopping Village.**

Coffelt Country Crossroads Shopping Village

This "hillbilly style" collection of businesses features craft stores, flea markets and gift shops. At Coffelt's you may even get to sit for a spell and enjoy the wandering musicians and singers who often come to entertain. If you would like dessert, pay a visit to the General Store for an ice cream cone or an old-fashioned soda.

The Way Back

This concludes today's trip. If you head uphill on 165 for half a mile, you'll be at the Strip. To get back to your starting point, you could turn right and travel 3½ miles east on 76. To avoid the traffic, however, it's best to follow one of the Time Saver Routes.

Travel Tips

- From Coffelt's Shopping Village, you can easily follow either the Blue or Yellow Time Saver Routes. To find the Yellow Route, travel up the hill a short way to the stoplight at Green Mountain Drive *(see map on page 84 or refer to the Yellow Route Map shown in Chapter One).*
- To find the Blue Route, follow 165 up the hill to Missouri 76, cross 76 (the road will become Gretna) and follow Gretna Rd. to Roark Valley Rd. *(refer to the Blue Route Map in Chapter One).*

Aerial view of Table Rock Lake.

Nearby

Historic

Towns

Car Tour #1

Rockaway Beach
Forsyth
Hollister

Car Tour #2

Reeds Spring
Branson West

Branson's Best

6

All the buildings along Hollister's Downing Street are listed in the National Register of Historic Places.

There's lots of history in these Ozark hills, and the best way to discover it is to travel to some of the hometown communities surrounding Branson. None are very far, and each will paint its own colorful picture of the area's rich and historic past.

There are two car tours in this chapter. One will guide you to Rockaway Beach, Forsyth and Hollister; the other tour will take you to Branson West and Reeds Spring. Flea markets and antique stores are always fun to explore, and you'll find them everywhere in Ozark Mountain Country. Included in the trips are directions to some of the larger operations, but if you really enjoy hunting for old-time treasures, keep a sharp lookout and stop at all you have time for.

Rockaway Beach, Forsyth and Hollister
Car Tour 1

History envelops these three old towns like an early-morning Ozark mist. During the Civil War, residents of Forsyth saw control of their city seesaw back and forth between the Confederate and Union armies. Just after the turn of the 20th century, the village of Hollister welcomed a new railroad carrying hoards of tourists, and in the Roaring '20s visitors to Rockaway Beach danced to the sounds of the big bands as they cruised the "new" Lake Taneycomo.

For an added treat on today's car tour, you could plan on a country breakfast in Rockaway Beach—it's about a 15-minute drive from Branson.

How To Get There

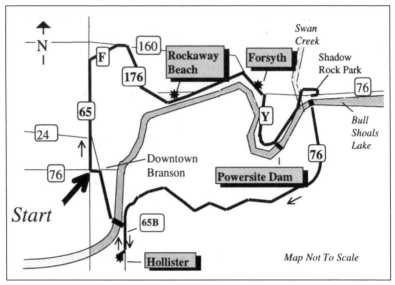

Approximate round-trip mileage: 37.

From the **U.S. 65** and **Missouri 76** intersection, travel north on U.S. 65 for about five miles to **Route F** (exit 16). Turn right on F, heading east, and follow it for almost three miles until it meets Missouri 160/176. Turn right and travel about two blocks to where Missouri 176 takes off to the right. Turn right and follow 176 all the way to **Rockaway Beach** (about two and one-half miles). Watch the highway signs closely to be sure you stay on 176. After about a mile and a half, 176 will make a sharp right turn and Highway EE will head straight. If you inadvertently take Highway EE, you could bypass the town.

As you head down the hill toward town, Lake Taneycomo will come into view along with many of the comfortable Mom-and-Pop resorts built during the city's golden days. On the lakefront, just after the road curves, you'll see a long walkway heading out to an island. Before Table Rock Dam changed the lake's temperature, this area was used as the "bathing island." Today it sports a popular public pier where you can fish or just relax and enjoy the view. If you would like to walk to the end of the pier, the parking area is easy to spot.

A few blocks farther, in the center of town, you'll find a cafe, deli and flea markets.

Rockaway Beach (pop. 275)

Life is slow and easy in Rockaway. Longtime residents usually meet for coffee at the local cafe to discuss the weather, politics, old dogs and the way things used to be. Down on the lakefront, trout anglers fish from a redwood dock while ducks and geese glide and bob between their lines.

In Rockaway's good old days, the town wasn't nearly this quiet. After Kansas City businessman Willard Merriam founded the community in 1915, Rockaway Beach quickly became a swinging summer hot spot for well-off vacationers from Kansas City and St. Louis. In those days, because there were no roads leading to Rockaway, travelers disembarking from trains at either

There's nothing like a peaceful day of fishing on Lake Taneycomo.

the Branson or Hollister depots had to complete their journey by boat. After arriving in Rockaway, however, they found first-class accommodations at luxury hotels and resorts.

During the day, visitors spent their time fishing, swimming or sunbathing on "Velvet Beach"—so named because of its soft, pebble-free shore. In the evening, guests could take nighttime dance cruises. It was the era of jazz, and as turn-of-the-century paddlewheels floated lazily up Lake Taneycomo, the music of Louis Armstrong could be heard echoing across the Ozark hills.

In the 1920s the Ozarks also echoed the country's resistance to Prohibition, and visitors coming to Rockaway during that time could always get a sample of the hill folks' moonshine "likker." Chicago gangster Al Capone was rumored to have been a frequent guest of the festive resort town.

Rockaway remained a popular vacation destination until the 1960s. The construction of Table Rock Dam was partly responsible for its decline. After the dam was built in 1959, the frigid (48-degree) water pouring into Taneycomo from the bottom of Table Rock Lake destroyed Taneycomo's native warm-water fishery. Anglers who had been coming to the area for many years could no longer fish their favorite holes for bass, perch or catfish, and their families could no longer use the lake for water skiing or swimming. Although trout fishing has come to the forefront, bringing new anglers, the area has never fully recovered.

Today, because of its proximity to Branson, residents of Rockaway are working hard to revitalize the town in hopes of once again attracting visitors to its quaint and quiet amenities.

Restaurants

Our suggestion for breakfast is **The Hillside Inn**, featuring a traditional country breakfast at reasonable prices.

Two flea markets, **Wild Goose Gifts** and **Captain Ed's Antiques**, are located across from the Hillside Inn. In the 1920s the long gray building housing both markets and the Elks lodge was a huge dance pavilion. Boats filled with revelers from Branson came to Rockaway to spend their evenings dancing in the pavilion overlooking the lake.

When ready to leave Rockaway Beach, continue traveling northeast on Missouri 176. As you head uphill, you'll see an unusual rock home (on the right) with a pagoda-style roof. "Whylaway," as the home was called when Willard Merriam built it in 1920, still looks much the same as when it was new.

When you reach the fork in the road **(Highway EE)**, just outside of town, be sure to veer to the right and follow 176 along the shoreline and then uphill until it joins again with **Missouri 160**. Turn right and head east for two miles to Forsyth.

On the way into town is a scenic overlook worth stopping for. Down below the lofty cliff you'll see Lake Taneycomo meandering its way through the hills. Taneycomo, technically a lake because it has a dam at both ends, still resembles a river as it follows the original path of the White River. The White was a vital transportation corridor for the region's early settlers in the 19th century. The peaceful community of Long Beach is on the other side of the lake.

Forsyth (pop. 1,100)

Today, the town of Forsyth sits safe and secure atop a hill overlooking Bull Shoals Lake, with nothing much to disturb its comfortable existence—except maybe in the early spring when the white bass start running. But the quiet community (founded as the seat of government for Taney County in 1837) hasn't always had it so easy.

When it was founded, the town wasn't even located where it is now. The settlement's early residents built their village about a quarter of a mile away, at the confluence of Swan Creek and the White River. During the years that it sat near the river, severe flooding was a constant threat. Residents never knew when their homes would be inundated with the rising waters of the mighty White. In 1861, however, something even more devastating than the river was about to overpower the small town—the Civil War.

During the war Forsyth became a central point of conflict between the North and the South. Occupation of the town shifted back and forth several times, until at the end Union troops set fire to the village just to keep it out of Confederate hands. By 1863 nothing was left of the town but the burned-out shell of the courthouse.

Times remained difficult for residents in the years after the war. Bushwhackers and outlaws wandered the hills, and friction between residents who had fought on opposite sides during the war sometimes became violent. It was during this volatile time that a gang called the Bald Knobbers began roaming the hills around Forsyth. Although the Bald Knobbers had originally been established as a peacekeeping force, the community soon came to fear the very vigilante committee that had been organized for their protection. Those who spoke out against the group's actions were roughly reprimanded—or sometimes just disappeared.

Bald Knobber. *Photo courtesy of Shepherd of the Hills Homestead.*

A view of Lake Taneycomo from the scenic overlook in Forsyth.

Hand-hewn log cabin in Shadow Rock Park.

To combat the outlaws, a small band of citizens formed their own gang. They called themselves the Anti-Baldknobbers, and began to plot the demise of the ruthless leader of the Bald Knobbers—Nat Kinney. The fearsome leader stood 6 feet 6, weighed more than 300 pounds, and at one time had more than 500 loyal followers. After Nat Kinney's death in 1888—at the hands of the Anti-Baldknobbers—peace finally came to the region.

Forsyth remained peaceful until late in the 1940s, when the community was forced to face a new enemy. This time the foe was progress. In 1947, after the U.S. Army Corps of Engineers announced the construction of Bull Shoals Dam near Mountain Home, Arkansas, the residents of Forsyth were told that they would have to move the town to make way for the new lake. In 1950 the entire city was relocated to the top of Shadow Rock Mountain. Today, this tenacious town, having survived more than its share of adversities, is a growing community attracting tourists and new residents who appreciate its old-fashioned small-town charm.

Follow Missouri 160 to the traffic light at **Co. Rd. Y**. (Later you're going to take Rd. Y to Powersite Dam.) Forsyth doesn't have any major tourist attractions (besides the historic dam), but if you would like to see its quaint old business district, turn left (east) at the Missouri 160 and Rd. Y intersection. You'll be on **David St.** heading uphill toward **Main St.** Main runs a very short distance to the right and left. Many of the old buildings along Main were moved to this site when the town was relocated. If you take Main to the left, you'll return to Missouri 160. If you take it to the right, you'll have to turn right at **Short St.** to return to 160.

There are a variety of restaurants near the 160/Y intersection. **The Fox and Turtle** (in the strip center just north of Rd. Y on Missouri 160) offers burgers, sandwiches and plate lunches at hometown prices. Burgers, hot dogs, soft-serve ice cream, shakes and sundaes can be found at the **Forsyth Drive-In** located a block west on Rd. Y.

A Sunday afternoon picnic near Forsyth (photo taken around 1915). *Photo courtesy of Branson Tri-Lakes Daily News.*

Next on today's trip is **Powersite Dam**, just a few miles west of Forsyth. To find the dam, head west on Co. Rd. Y. After circling along the ridge top, the road will head downhill and lead you to Empire Electric Park. This pretty public park is popular year-round for picnicking, fishing and camping. The dam is a short distance from the park, and just past the dam is a convenient lookout point. Bull Shoals Lake begins on the low side of the dam, and Lake Taneycomo ends on the high side.

Powersite Dam

Construction of the dam began in 1911 and was finished two years later. After completion, the historic dam (546 feet wide and 70 feet high) was one of the nation's largest privately owned dams operated exclusively for the generation of hydroelectric power. Powersite (originally called the Ozark Beach Dam) became a popular meeting place for ice cream socials and picnic-basket suppers by the lake.

For a closer look at the dam, follow Road Y from the lookout point for a short distance to the end of the fence row (on
the right). Turn right, and follow the gravel road back toward
the dam to the water's edge. During high water Lake
Taneycomo spills over the dam, but when the water level is
low you won't see much in the way of an impressive waterfall. The area is still a good place to stretch your legs and
search for an interesting rock or piece of driftwood.

When ready to leave the dam, continue following Co. Rd.
Y along the lowlands (don't take any roads off to the left) to
the bridge that spans Swan Creek. In the nineteenth century
an Indian trading post was located near this site. After crossing the Swan Creek bridge, turn left and follow the road
heading under the higher bridge.

Shadow Rock Park

Flood-prone Shadow Rock Park is where the town square
was located before the village was moved to make way for
the new lake. To find the site of the old courthouse, travel
past the picnic area and turn right at the road leading to the
rustic log cabin. Local residents constructed the partly furnished hand-hewn log cabin by using materials collected
from several homes in the area. The two commemorative
plaques, to the right of the cabin, will give you more of
Forsyth's historic highlights.

When ready to leave the park, follow the main road uphill and
turn right. Turn right again at the stop sign at **Missouri 160/76**.
Travel to the bridge and turn left, crossing Bull Shoals Lake. You're
now on **Missouri 76** heading west toward Branson and Hollister.
It's about 13 miles to Hollister.

Powersite Dam.

Along the way, in the town of Kirbyville, is The Ozark Mountaineer Magazine and Book Shop (on the left). The Ozark Mountaineer, open Monday through Friday, specializes in books about Ozark history, folklore, cooking, and music.

When you get to the stoplight at the Taneycomo Bridge (Downtown Branson is on the other side of the lake), continue driving straight (you're now on **Business 65/Veterans Boulevard**) and travel one mile to **Downing Street** (it will veer off to the right, paralleling the railroad tracks).

Hollister (pop. 2628)

Like Branson, Hollister became a popular tourist destination after the St. Louis Iron Mountain and Southern Railway chugged its way through the area in 1906. The main attraction was camping and fishing along the White River.

In its heyday, as many as nine excursion trains a day dropped well-to-do passengers at the Hollister depot. Seeking to draw tourists, the city's early planners mandated that all new buildings be constructed in the English Tudor style of architecture. Travelers of yesteryear were, no doubt, as surprised to find an Old English village in the middle of the Ozarks as is today's visitor.

In those early years, Hollister was a thriving agricultural mecca, surrounded by stockyards, vineyards, orchards, tobacco fields, and cotton farms. The town is noted for leading the way in community development in the Ozarks. It had the area's first paved streets, electric lights, movie house, iron bridge (still in use) and a modern steam-heated hotel known as **Ye English Inn.**

Ye English Inn, still the grandest building in town, has undergone many changes since it was completed in 1909. A 1927 newspaper editorial described it as being equal to the best metropolitan hotels. The inn featured hot and cold water and, according to the article, "snowy napery, delicate chinaware and glistening glassware and silver that affords an atmosphere of elegance." The gracious inn and the city of Hollister, however, were about to fall on hard times.

The invention of the automobile, the Great Depression and a new highway that bypassed the city (U.S. 65)—all played a part in Hollister's decline, as did the constant flooding of the White River. Ye English Inn closed its doors in 1945 after a flood deposited nearly nine feet of water in the lobby. By 1955 the only businesses remaining in town were the post office and grocery.

The threat of flooding ended after the construction of Table Rock Dam, and the town began a slow recovery. Local investors renovated and reopened the inn, and new businesses began lining Downing Street. Today, because of its quaint romantic charm and nearness to Branson, Hollister is once again attracting its share of tourists. Most are coming by car, but the depot is seeing activity again as trains from Houston, Dallas and San Antonio, Texas, are once again bringing visitors to the area.

Hollister is a quiet little town compared to Branson; you can park anywhere along the street and stroll leisurely from shop to shop. Downing St. is registered as a National Historic District, and each near-century-old building has its own commemorative plaque.

Some Downing Street Shops

Shops come and go along Downing Street, but two that have stayed awhile are **The Flea Collar Antique Mall** and **Green Lantern Antiques.** The first is a huge air-conditioned flea market (perfect for browsing on a hot summer day), and the second is a dusty old shop filled with everything from delicate china to rusty farm tools.

Across the railroad tracks is the Mo-Pac Train Depot, built in 1910. Next to it is a fire-engine-red caboose reminiscent of Hollister's railroad days. Today, the depot is home to the Hollister Chamber of Commerce. If you would like more information about the area, stop in pay them a visit. They have several history books written by locals available for sale.

The Way Back

This concludes today's car tour. To get back to the starting point, follow Downing Street back to Business 65 and turn left. Travel one mile to the Taneycomo Bridge, turn left (crossing the lake) and follow Business 65/E. Missouri 76 to Main Street in Downtown Branson. Turn left on Main (Missouri 76) and travel uphill to U.S. 65.

Old time treasures are tucked into every nook and cranny of Green Lantern Antiques in Hollister.

Reeds Springs and Branson West
Car Tour 2

Reeds Spring, settled in the late 19th century as a logging center, is better known today as an art community. Many of the town's resident artisans create and display their work in their own shops along the streets of the century-old town. You'll even find a few fine art galleries—a bit unusual for these parts. Branson West, one of the area's newer communities, was founded in 1974 to accommodate the many tourists visiting the Table Rock Lake area. Talking Rocks Cavern, a popular tourist attraction, is near Branson West. This car tour has an abundance of flea markets and collectible shops.

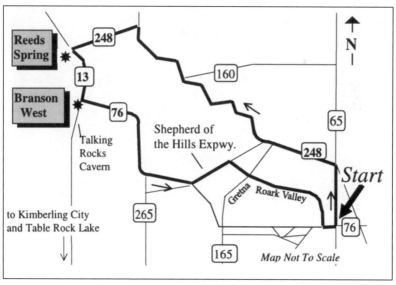

Approximate round trip mileage: 36.

How To Get There

Reeds Spring is about 14 miles west of Branson. From the **U.S. 65** and **Missouri 76** intersection, head north on U.S. 65 for one mile to **Missouri 248/Shepherd of the Hills Expressway**. Head west (left) on Missouri 248 for almost 14 miles (**U.S. 160** will join 248 and the road will be marked as both) to Reeds Spring Junction.

Potter Mark Oehler at work in his pottery shop in Reeds Spring

Turn left and follow Missouri 248 for about two miles before you begin looking on the left for **Mark Oehler's Omega Pottery Shop** (just inside the city limits). For more than 20 years Mark has been decorating, glazing and kiln-firing heirloom-quality wheel-thrown pottery in his studio behind the gallery.

When ready to continue, turn left and follow 248 to the stop sign at **Missouri 13/265**. If you would like to visit another potter, turn right and travel about one mile to **Hess' Pottery Shop**. The shop is housed in a Mongolian yurt—a circular domed structure that somehow seems to remain cool even on the hottest days. Tom Hess designs his pottery from natural terra cotta clay, and his wife, Lory Brown, weaves intricately patterned, one-of-a-kind baskets from yellow pine needles.

To find the way to downtown Reeds Spring, retrace your way back to Missouri 248 and continue heading south on 13 for a short distance to the center of town. A convenient parking lot is on the left between **Bass Pro Shop** and **Old Spring Flea Market**.

Reeds Springs (pop. 411)

Like Branson and Hollister, Reeds Spring profited greatly by the coming of the railroad. Before the track could be laid, however, a quarter-mile tunnel had to be blasted through a mountain east of town. In 1902 a railroad camp was established, and workers came from all over the country to drill the tunnel.

Starting at opposite ends of the mountain, it took the two crews four years to reach the middle. Amazingly, when they met they were only a fraction of an inch off center. After the tunnel was completed, many crewmembers chose to stay in Reeds Spring. Historians record these early residents as "hard-working, hard-drinking and hard-fighting folk."

As railroads began expanding across the Southwest, there

was a great demand for timber to be converted into railroad ties. Even before the St. Louis Iron Mountain and Southern Railway made its way to the Ozarks in 1906, huge oaks were being harvested from the vast timberland covering the region. After logs were cut into ties—by workers called hackers—they were lashed into huge rafts and floated down the James River to markets in Arkansas.

The railroad brought a faster and more efficient method of hauling ties to market, and until about 1925 Reeds Spring was the largest supplier of white oak ties in the US. After that time, most of the area's virgin forests were depleted and the once lucrative logging trade ended.

Reeds Spring's most infamous visitors came to town in 1932. While running from the law, Bonnie Parker and Clyde Barrow (Bonnie and Clyde) stopped just long enough to kidnap a Reeds Spring resident to use as a hostage before leaving town in a blaze of gunfire. The man was later released unharmed in Arkansas.

Main Street

Old Spring Flea Market (in the center of the street) is the spring that gave life to the town. In the 19th century, cattle ranchers driving their herds north from Texas and Oklahoma often used this cool, flowing Ozark spring as a resting place. Legend has it that on a cattle drive from Texas in the 1870s the Reed brothers discovered the beauty of the area and became the first homesteaders to settle permanently near the spring. During the building of the railroad tunnel the spring supplied about a million gallons of water a day to power the workers' steam-powered drills.

Among the shops on Main Street is the the **New Coast Gallery**. At the New Coast Gallery you'll find a diversified selection of jewelry, copper work, mobiles, photography, and paintings.

Antiques like this beautiful old doll are plentiful in the Reeds Spring area.

Restaurants

If you would like a chili dog or a burrito, try **Pop's Dari Dell**, north on Missouri 13 (just before the stop sign at Missouri 248). Pop's also serves sundaes, shakes, and soft-serve ice cream. You'll find a country-style cafe called **The Hungry Hunter** as you head out of town. Their full-service menu includes burgers, plate lunches, sandwiches, and salads.

When ready to leave the main shopping district, follow Missouri 13 south for one block and make a stop at the **Sawdust Doll**. This shop features paintings, sculptures and dolls by artisan

Kay Cloud, whose century-old technique of doll making has been featured in many country art magazines. Across the street from the Sawdust Doll is the distinctive estate of Joe Dan Dwyer, born and raised in a small house on this site. After he was injured in a logging accident up north, Dwyer returned to his birthplace to build the existing home and unusual gardens.

Turn right as you leave the Sawdust Doll and travel a short way south to **The Old Barn** (on the left). Standing on this site since about 1905, the rustic red barn is now a flea market and collectible shop.

Turn left when you're ready to leave The Old Barn and head south. Just outside of Reeds Spring, **Missouri 76** will join **Missouri 13** and the route will be marked as **13/76/265** (the Hungry Hunter restaurant is on the right just after this junction). It's about three miles to Branson West from this junction.

About midway is **Robbins Antiques** (on the left). Along with vintage collectibles and some of the best country-cured bacon you'll ever taste, they carry homemade jams, jellies and preserves—blackberry and peach are the favorites, but you'll also find such unusual varieties as gooseberry and strawberry-rhubarb.

Branson West (pop. 37)

Branson West, stationed at the turn in the road that steers travelers to Silver Dollar City and Branson, is a newcomer compared to most Ozark towns. When it was incorporated as a village in 1974, twenty-eight people from approximately fourteen families were on hand to sign a petition to name the new town Lakeview.

As more and more tourists discovered this back door to Branson, Lakeview grew busy enough to warrant a shopping center, a McDonald's, and a Wal-Mart Super Center. In the

The Old Barn antique shop in Reeds Spring.

early '90s controversy occurred when the city's leaders proposed to change the town's name from Lakeview to Branson West. When implemented, the new name eliminated having two Lakeviews in the state of Missouri, and also allowed the community to take advantage of the tremendous amount of publicity being generated by their illustrious neighbor.

Kimberling City and Table Rock Lake are about six miles south of Branson West on Missouri 13. This resort-rich region is popular with families and anglers because of its easy access to the lake and all outdoor activities. In November and December, Kimberling City presents a huge holiday lighting display called the "Port of Lights." If visiting during the Christmas season, be sure to take time to see it.

Your next stop is at a delightful country crafts shop located just east of Branson West, unless you would like to visit one of the area's caves. **Talking Rocks Cavern** (Telephone: (417) 272-3366) is just a short distance south of town. If you would like to make it part of today's trip, continue driving south on Missouri 13 and look on the left for a huge boulder showing you where to turn. The attraction features a 45-minute guided tour. Admission range for adults is $11.95, children 5 to 12 are $5.95, and kids 4 and under go free.

If you're not going to visit the cave, turn left (east) on **Missouri 76** (at the stoplight just past Wal-Mart.) About two miles from town (on the right across from the Phillips 66 gas station), you'll find the crafts shop.

The Ozark Mountain Craft Village

Char DeMoro, the store's owner, designs country-style fabric gift items for Silver Dollar City, the Cracker Barrel restaurant chain and other businesses across the country. Lining the shop's shelves are whimsical dolls, teddy bears, rabbits, angels, quilts and other items created by Char and other local crafters. Next to the craft shop is **Stone Creek Crossing,** a store filled with unusual decorative items and gifts.

The Way Back

When you're ready to continue, turn right and head east on Missouri 76. You could follow Missouri 76 all the way back to your starting point, but to avoid the traffic on the Strip it's better to use one of the Time Saver Routes. The map at the beginning of this trip follows the Shepherd of the Hills Expressway (the Red Route) to Roark Valley Road (the Blue Route). Roark Valley will connect with W. Missouri 76 near U.S. 65.

Enchanting Eureka Springs

Christ of the Ozarks Statue

The Crescent Hotel

Queen Anne Mansion

Downtown Shopping District

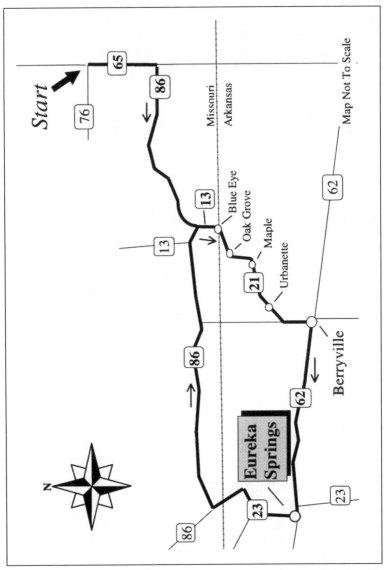

Eureka Springs, Arkansas. *Approximate round-trip mileage: 100.*

The spirited word "Eureka" means "I've found it," and for over a hundred years visitors have been finding this storybook city in the Ozark hills. *Time* magazine calls it "A Victorian National Treasure" because it offers the largest collection of 19th-century homes in the central United States. A visit to Eureka Springs, Arkansas, is like stepping into a Victorian fairytale, and it's only a one-hour drive from Branson.

On your trip today, you'll be guided to this historic town and those attractions that best represent its "old-world" charm–all at very little cost. You'll tour a magnificent century-old home, ride an old-time trolley, and discover quaint shops, churches, hotels and restaurants.

What to See and Do

- **Big Cedar Lodge**—one of Branson's finest resorts.
- **Christ of the Ozarks Statue**—a giant 7-story inspirational landmark located on the grounds of the Passion Play Complex.
- **Queen Anne Mansion**—a majestic, immaculately restored, 19th-century manor.
- **Eureka Springs Trolley**—a journey into the 19th century along tree-shaded streets lined with gingerbread-trimmed homes, manicured lawns and flower-filled gardens.

- **Crescent Hotel**—a towering 19th-century hostelry reminiscent of a time of quiet elegance.
- **St. Elizabeth's Catholic Church**—a hundred-year-old chapel listed in *Ripley's Believe It or Not* as the only church entered by way of the bell tower.
- **The Historic Shopping District**—a place to wander and explore streets crowded with European-style shops, art galleries, historic hotels and picturesque parks.

Tips, Tactics & Timesavers!

- Grab a quick breakfast and leave as early as possible. Although Eureka is only a one-hour drive from Branson, there's a full day of activities ahead and you'll want to have plenty of time to enjoy all the city has to offer.
- Eureka's narrow, winding streets were built for the horse and buggy, not the automobile. The best way to get around town is to ride the trolley. Directions are given on where to park your car and where to board the trolley.
- The trolley operates daily April through October. From November 1 to December 14, it operates only on weekends. During the rest of the year, you can pick up a map at the Visitor and Information Center and travel by car.
- Wear comfortable clothing and walking shoes. There's lots of old-world ambiance along Eureka's streets, and walking is the best way to experience it.
- Take your camera. You'll want to capture all the beauty of this lovely city on film.

How To Get There

The first attraction on today's trip is a quick drive-through tour of **Big Cedar Lodge**. From the **U.S. 65** and **Missouri 76** intersection, take U.S. 65 south for nine miles to **Missouri 86**. Turn right (west) on 86, and drive about half a mile to the Big Cedar entrance at **Devil's Pool Road.** Turn right and head down the hill for almost two miles. Although you're not going to stop at the lodge, it's worth the short trip just to see this beautiful resort overlooking Table Rock Lake. Big Cedar, owned by Bass Pro Shops, is listed in *Midwest Living* as one of its "50 Top Vacation Destinations."

After traveling down the hill, look on the right for a rustic Big Cedar Lodge sign with a Bass Pro Shops logo located *above* a narrow one-way roadway. The road will circle through heavy woods, cross flowing streams, and deliver you to a rustic four-story lodge building overlooking the lake. Follow the road as it heads down the hill to the registration building. You may want to return at another time to dine at the lodge's restaurants, visit the gift shop, or take a horseback ride. *(The car tour in Chapter Ten includes more complete information about the lodge and restaurant.)*

To return to Missouri 86 from the lodge, follow the exit signs to the main road. Turn left and head up the hill. When you reach 86, turn right and travel about twelve miles to **Missouri 13**. At this junction, continue driving straight to continue traveling south on 13. (Don't turn right or you'll be on 86/13 heading west.)

It's just one mile to the town of **Blue Eye**, a small village straddling the Missouri-Arkansas state line. In the center of town, after crossing the state line, Missouri 13 will become Arkansas **Highway 21**.

Follow 21 toward **Oak Grove** and **Maple**. The gently rolling countryside along this stretch of highway displays pastoral views of peaceful farms, grazing livestock and fields of wildflowers. Common Ozark wildflowers include Queen

Anne's Lace, goldenrod, spiderwort, columbine, sweet William, trumpet creeper, and black-eyed Susan.

After making a right turn at the stop sign in Oak Grove, it's about 4 miles farther to Maple, where **Cosmic Caverns** is located. Because there's so much to see and do in Eureka Springs, the cavern isn't included on today's trip, but since this is your vacation, you might prefer to spend the time here. *The guided one-third-mile tour lasts about one hour, and admission is in the $10 range for adults and $6 for children over four.*

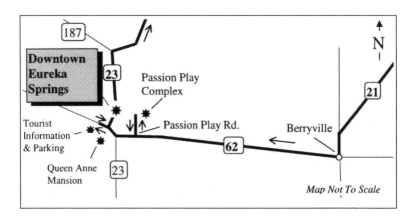

Continue traveling on 21, through Urbanette, to the historic town of **Berryville** *(a visit to Berryville is included in the car tour in Chapter Ten)*. In Berryville, turn right (west) on **Highway 62**, and travel eleven miles to **Passion Play Road**. You'll see a large billboard on the right directing you where to turn just inside the city limits of **Eureka Springs**.

Turn right and travel one mile to the **Passion Play Complex**. The Great Passion Play (the story of the life, death, resurrection and ascension of Jesus Christ) is performed only in the evenings, but there are several daytime attractions. Your first stop is the **Christ of the Ozarks Statue**.

To reach the statue, follow the main road past the parking area and ticket office. Continue following it as it circles to the left, heads downhill past the **Church in the Grove**, and ends at the parking area below the statue. From this spot you can stroll to the statue and back to the church. There's no charge to view these attractions.

In the early 1960s Mr. and Mrs. Gerald Smith were inspired by their faith to create an outdoor site where people could gather to celebrate the life of Christ. Their first project was to design and build the towering statue on the hill. The seven-story sculpture, weighing over one million pounds, has an arm span of 65 feet. From the lookout point below the statue, you can see Eureka Springs on the far hillside.

When ready, you can walk or drive to the church. The pretty whitewashed chapel, originally built in 1905, was moved here from a rural community in northwest Arkansas. Because Eureka Springs is well known as a wedding mecca, the little backwoods church is booked throughout the year by couples seeking a nostalgic "country-style" ceremony. Many

Christ of the Ozarks Statue in Eureka Springs
Photo courtesy of the Elna M. Smith Foundation

of the town's lodging facilities cater to honeymooners, and you'll see many romantic and cozy bed-and-breakfasts all along the tree-shaded streets of Eureka's residential district.

Next to the church, an authentic ten-foot section of the **Berlin Wall** bears graffiti in German paraphrasing the twenty-third Psalm. After the fall of the Berlin Wall in 1989, this exceptional remnant was transported from Germany to the Port of Houston, and from there it was delivered by truck to Eureka Springs.

When ready to leave the church, drive back up the hill and park in any lot near the ticket office. From here you can walk behind the ticket office building to view the **Amphitheater** and the old-world set where the **Passion Play** is presented. In the last twenty-five years, over five million visitors have seen the "City of Old Jerusalem" come to life with a cast of two hundred actors, plus live camels, sheep, donkeys, and doves. *Time* magazine has described the presentation as "among the best the country has to offer."

> The play is presented from the end of April to the end of October. If you would like additional information regarding times and dates, ask at the ticket office or call (800) 882-PLAY. Web site:www.greatpassionplay.com

If it's open, you can also visit the **Smith Memorial Chapel**, the large white circular building located across the street from the amphitheater. It features a 15th century hand-carved Dutch altar and religious art.

This concludes the tour of the complex's free attractions. There are several other attractions that charge a nominal admission fee. The **Sacred Arts Center** (located to the left of the ticket office) exhibits oil paintings, sculptures, ivory carvings, and other Christian art. The **Bible Museum** (located below the Smith Chapel) houses many rare Bibles and religious manuscripts. The **New Holy Land Tour** is a two-hour narrated trip by bus to settings depicting such biblical sites as Christ's Tomb, the Last Supper and the Nativity. Due to the length of the tour it's not included on today's trip, but if you prefer to spend the time here, check at the **Orientation Center** for times and prices. The Orientation Center also has a large religious gift shop.

When ready to leave the complex, follow Passion Play Road back to Highway 62, turn right, and head into town. It's about three slow, curvy miles to the parking area. "Little Switzerland of America" is a phrase often used to describe Eureka Springs, and throughout the city you'll see many businesses designed to capture the romantic look of that old-world country.

How to Get Around

The best way to visit Eureka Springs is to park your car and ride the trolley.

Parking spaces are at a premium here, and all the lots in town charge for parking. A convenient and reasonably priced lot is at the **Visitor Information Center** on Highway 62 (the road you're traveling on). To find the visitor center, follow 62 past the point where Highway 23 joins it from the left (for a short distance the road will be marked as both). Continue following 62 past the junction where 23 takes off to the right, heading toward downtown. On the other side of the intersection, on the left, you'll see the **Queen Anne Mansion** perched majestically on the hill. Just down from it, on the left, is the entrance to the visitor center (look for the bright green gates). It's easy to miss the entrance, so be sure to drive slowly after passing the Queen Anne.

After parking, check the number of your parking space and deposit the parking fee in the same numbered slot in the yellow collection box at the top of the hill. If you need change, you can get it at the visitor center, where you're going next to buy tickets for the trolley.

For today's visit, you'll want to buy an "all-day" ticket, which allows you to get off and on the trolley as many times as you wish without an additional charge. It is $3.50 for the all-day ticket. Children six and under go free. *Keep your ticket handy; you'll need it each time you're ready to reboard.*

Along with your ticket, you'll receive a copy of the **Trolley Map and Area Attractions Guide**. You may want to take a minute to look over the map, which will give you an idea of how the village is designed, where the attractions are, and what color trolley route will get you there. Each trolley will have a matching color sign, either in the window or on the bumper, indicating the route it will take. On today's trip, you'll be touring only the Red Route through Eureka's historic residential and downtown districts.

Also available at the information center is a $2 walking guide. In it are six walking tours (with maps) of the downtown area. Besides the six tours, it has wonderful vintage photos and historical information. If it's your first time here, however, you might want to save a walking tour for another visit.

To understand how a city such as Eureka came to be, and why it looks today much the same as it did in the nineteenth century, here's a look at its unusual history.

Eureka Springs (pop. 1,900)

The hills surrounding Eureka contain more than 60 flowing springs. Indians living in the area in the 19th century believed that the pure mineral water gushing from the abundant springs brought good health, and they passed the legend on to the white settlers.

An early pioneer doctor named Alvah Jackson began sending patients to the springs for treatment. Word spread, and it wasn't long before hundreds came seeking a cure for whatever ailed them. In 1879, a settlement was founded and makeshift tents were set up to house the health seekers.

When the railroad arrived in 1883, visitors began flocking to the little town. Physicians and bankers took up residence and eager entrepreneurs began building grand hotels and restaurants to accommodate the mostly wealthy travelers. The town's successful businessmen were able to build extravagant homes and surround them with beautifully landscaped gardens. Soon, stylish vacationers were coming from all over the world to enjoy Eureka's elegant lodgings and fashionable bathhouses. The city's charms included streets illuminated by gas lights, electrified trolley cars and band concerts in the park.

After medical science reversed the belief in the spring water's medicinal powers, the city's popularity declined. Without funds to rebuild and refurbish buildings and streets, the town remained the same and so did the grace and elegance of a bygone era. Today, vacationers no longer come

1895 photo of Eureka Springs. *Photo courtesy of Bank of Eureka Springs.*

to Eureka seeking a health cure; they come to enjoy the beauty and graciousness of a living keepsake of the past.

What To See First

The first "don't miss" attraction in town is the lovely old mansion you just passed, and it's only a short walk from the visitor center.

The Queen Anne Mansion

Telephone: (800) MANSION

The Queen Anne Mansion (open from 10 A.M. to 5 P.M.) is an AAA star-rated attraction that has been featured in *Southern Living* and *Victorian Homes* magazines. There are two historic homes on this site and you can visit either or both, but the one not to miss is the Queen Anne. *Admission for adults is $6; children (seven to thirteen) are charged $3.50 and those six and under go free.*

The lavish three-story, 12,000-square-foot Victorian home was originally built in Carthage, Missouri (in 1891), for $21,500. In 1984 it was moved piece by piece to Eureka Springs at a cost of over half a million dollars. Each room is fully decorated with period antique furnishings and accessories. Be sure to note the home's remarkable woodwork, shown best in its seven hand-carved fireplace mantels and five pocket doors (doors that slide into the walls). A free pamphlet summarizing the home's history is available at the ticket desk.

When ready to leave the mansion and continue your tour of Eureka Springs, walk to the **Trolley Stop** in front of the Queen Anne and board whatever trolley comes along. From this point, all trolleys go to the main depot at the foot of Spring Street.

The Queen Anne Mansion. *Photo courtesy of Queen Anne Mansion.*

At the depot you can catch the **Red Route** trolley (if you're already on one, just remain seated). Trolleys run, on average, every 20 to 30 minutes and stop operating at either 5 or 7 P.M. (depending on the time of year). If you're visiting late in the day, be sure to ask the driver when the last trolley will be leaving the downtown depot. Warming: trolley routes can change at any time. Ask the driver if you have any questions.

The Trolley

Not only is it fun to ride the trolley, but it's also a great way to begin experiencing the magic of Eureka. The trolley has been part of the street scene here from the city's earliest days.

After arriving by rail, turn-of-the-century visitors would ride a trolley (at that time electric) to their hotels. No doubt Eureka's early visitors were as delighted by the charming city as you will be. Eureka's gingerbread-trimmed, multigabled homes are reminiscent of an era when houses were painted pastel colors and decorated with ornate woodwork. Many of the houses are authentically preserved to exacting details that include historically accurate colors of paint.

Some visitors may ride the trolley along the tree-shaded streets, gaze at the beautiful homes and think they've seen Eureka Springs—but they would be wrong. Just waiting to be discovered are classic hotels, historic churches, interesting shops, and art galleries. To find them, however, you have to get off the trolley. Don't worry about getting lost; just return to one of the designated stops and another trolley will be along shortly. As you circle up Spring Street, you'll be able to check out some of the shops you'll want to visit later, when you're on foot.

First Stop: The Crescent Hotel

For two "must see" attractions, exit the trolley when the driver announces you're at the **Crescent Hotel** and **St. Elizabeth's Catholic Church**. There's no charge to visit these attractions, and both will present you with a unique glimpse into Eureka's fascinating past. (The trolley will drop you off at the hotel's front entrance and pick you up at the same location.)

After its construction in 1886, the Crescent was labeled "the finest hostelry west of the Mississippi." During the Gay '90s the hotel catered to the wealthiest of Eureka's visitors, and with a little imagination you can almost visualize the well-to-do lady of the day descending the wide carpeted staircase on her way to an evening carriage ride or a stroll in the garden.

Focal points in the entryway include the hotel's original reception desk and the massive fireplace in the center of the lobby. Behind the fireplace is the hotel gift shop.

Photo of Crescent Hotel taken before the turn of the 20th century. *Photo courtesy of Bank of Eureka Springs.*

Do You Believe in Ghosts?

The Crescent has the uncommon distinction of being certified as "haunted." Four resident ghosts have reportedly been seen on more than one occasion during the hotel's long history. These ghosts are known as: the Man in Black (thought to have been a wealthy traveler); Michael (an Irish stonecutter who had helped in the hotel's construction); a young schoolgirl (who leaped to her death from the fourth-floor observation deck in the 1920s); and a nurse (during the 1930s the hotel became a hospital, and over the years a nurse has been seen pushing a gurney through the hallways).

The hotel's most famous resident was Morris the cat. Arriving in 1973, the ragtag yellow kitten soon became a favorite of hotel employees, and even had his own private entrance. Outlasting several of the hotel's owners, Morris was 21 years old when he died in October 1994.

For a picture-perfect view of the Christ of the Ozarks Statue, take the elevator to the fourth-floor observation deck.

This scene is even more striking in the fall, when the Ozark hills come alive with the fiery colors of autumn. Down below you'll see St. Elizabeth's Catholic Church, the next stop on your tour.

To get to the church, go back to the lobby and exit through the back door. From the patio, descend the steps to the right, cross the road, and walk through the church's detached bell tower. St. Elizabeth's is listed in *Ripley's Believe It or Not* as the only church entered by way of its bell tower.

St. Elizabeth's Catholic Church

This beautiful chapel, built in 1904, is a combination of three types of architectural design. Just after entering, you'll be in the Rotunda, which is Byzantine in style and was modeled after the famous St. Sophia Church in Istanbul, Turkey. The main chamber (where the altar is) is of Romanesque design. The ceiling has unique Gothic-style truss supports, and above the balcony are the chapel's beautiful Gothic rose windows. The altars, pews, balcony, and Stations of the Cross were all features of the original church.

Other points of interest include: the Crucifix above the main altar, the four illustrated panels in the dome, the light fixture in the Rotunda, and two statues in the Rotunda that predate the church by some twenty years.

Off the back patio is another scenic view of the Christ of the Ozarks Statue and a great spot for picture taking. The entrance to a religious gift shop is also located off the back patio.

Back at the Hotel

If you're ready for lunch, you can dine in the European elegance of the **Crystal Dining Room**—look for the menu posted near the entrance. There are many other restaurants in the downtown district. When ready to continue your tour of Eureka, return to the front steps of the hotel to board the next trolley.

After taking you through Eureka's picturesque residential

St. Elizabeth's Catholic Church. *Photo courtesy of Bank of Eureka Springs.*

district, the trolley will circle back toward the visitor center. Stay on the trolley until it takes you back to the main depot, where you'll get off and begin exploring on foot.

Eureka's Downtown Shopping District

The shopping district is a place to wander and browse the streets and alleyways of another place in time—the entire downtown area is listed in the National Register of Historic Places. Although we couldn't begin to describe all of Eureka's shops and restaurants (over 150), mentioned are a few unique places to visit. The most memorable, however, will be the special ones you discover on your own.

The best way to see most everything in the shopping district is to first walk south (left) on Main Street. The first point of interest is the **Bank of Eureka Springs**. Take a minute to peek inside to see what a bank lobby looked like in the 1800s. Up the hill, on the right, is the **Eureka Springs**

Historical Museum. For a small fee ($2.50 for adults), you can view photos and artifacts donated by area families. The museum is housed in the Calif House, built in 1889. This small building was once used as a general store, boarding house, and a family home all at the same time. Next to the museum is a spring, with a tiny park and springhouse. The spring originates in a cave behind Calif House. In the early days, a system of ducts circulated the cool air from the cave into the building.

When ready to continue, walk back downhill past the depot and the point where Spring Street veers off and heads uphill. Main was once called Mud Street. It was named that because in the early years a nearby stream kept a steady flow of mud running down it. In 1928 the street was raised to its present level, which is why you have to walk down steps to reach the first floor of some of the buildings. When commercial development ends (it's only a few blocks), turn around and head back to Spring Street.

To see all of the wonderful shops on Spring, the easiest way is to wander up one side and down the other. A good spot to walk to before crossing the street and heading back is the lovely **Crescent Spring.** The tranquil, flower-filled setting reflects the pride residents take in their picture-postcard community. The pretty gazebo here was built in 1885.

Near Crescent Spring is the Carnegie Public Library, built in 1910 from limestone left over after the construction of the Crescent Hotel. If it's open, venture inside and experience its old-world ambience.

Near the library, you'll find a little store called **Frog Fantasies**. This shop contains a 6,000-piece frog collection and frog collectibles. Eureka Springs hosts a convention each year just for fanatical frog fans.

On Spring Street you'll also see the charming **Harding Spring**. An old Indian legend inspired the name of the rock bluff towering above the spring, and you'll find the story of why it's called "Lover's Leap" on a nearby signpost.

Another place of interest is the **Palace Hotel Bathhouse**.

Palace Hotel Bathhouse. *Photo courtesy of Palace Hotel Bathhouse.*

In its heyday, the Palace was one of Eureka's most luxurious hotels, and it is the only operational bathhouse in the Ozarks today.

Just beyond the Post Office stop, Spring Street will make a sharp turn to the left. Just across the street is **The Hammond Museum of Bells and Collectabells Shop**. Besides silver, brass, glass, and every other type of bell and chime, the shop features (for a small charge) a bell museum with a priceless collection of bells from around the world.

As you stroll down Spring Street, take time to notice one of Eureka's oldest hotels. **The New Orleans** (63 Spring) has had several names during its long history. When it was built in 1892 it was called the Wadsworth, after its original owner. In the late nineteenth century the wealthy Mr. Wadsworth married a beautiful bareback rider whom he found performing with the circus. After their wedding, he brought his bride to Eureka, the most popular spa of the era. Together they built and operated the hotel until Wadsworth's death. The hotel then became known as the Allred. During that time the inn advertised sixty luxurious rooms at the rate of $2.50 per night. It was later renamed the Springs and retained that name until 1984, when it was completely renovated and given its present name. It now offers eighteen elegant suites completely furnished with antiques from the Victorian era.

Located in the New Orleans is **The Imagery** photo shop, where you can get your picture taken in nineteenth century costumes. This is one souvenir that's sure to capture the essence of Eureka.

If you're a miniature collector, be sure to stop at **Happy Things** (55 Spring). It specializes in furniture, figurines, and anything you might want for collector boxes and dollhouses.

For a casual and inexpensive place to have lunch, check out **The Eureka Food Court** (37 Spring). The menu includes sandwiches, Mexican and American food, salads, and desserts. At 47 Spring Street is the **Sidewalk Café**, another place easy on the budget. They serve pizza, hot dogs, sandwiches, and salads.

As you near the bottom of the hill, look on the right for another historic hotel, the **Basin Park**. This hotel, built in

1905, is listed in *Ripley's Believe It or Not* as the only hotel in the world with access to all seven of its stories on a different ground floor. To see how this can be, take the elevator in the lobby to the fifth floor and follow either exit sign to the back door. Don't shut the door behind you; there's no knob on the outside. From here, you can see that each floor has a separate fire escape that connects to the hillside ascending straight up behind the entire seven-story hotel.

A special place to have lunch is right here in the Basin Park. **The Balcony Bar and Restaurant** has a balcony where you can savor Eureka's old-world atmosphere while you dine. The balcony is also a great location to take a picture of the triangular-shaped **Flatiron** building located across the street. The Flatiron is the most photographed building in Eureka Springs.

Flatiron III

The first European-style Flatiron was built on this site around 1880, but burned near the turn of the century. It was quickly rebuilt, but in 1929 it was again destroyed by fire. The current building was completed in 1988. Lower floors are used for retail shops and upper levels are used as guest quarters.

More Restaurants

Here are a few more restaurants located near the center of town. **DeVito's** (5 Center) offers fine dining and award-winning Italian specialties. **Basin Block Café** (established in 1896 and located across from the Basin Park Hotel) offers country-style fare; and the **Hole in the Wall** has southwestern-style cuisine. Check the menus posted in storefront windows for prices and daily specials.

Basin Circle Park

Basin Circle Park (next to the Basin Park Hotel) is a good spot to relax and do some people watching. The town of Eureka grew around Basin Spring. Looking across the street, you'll see the Basin Bath House, rebuilt in 1986 after a fire destroyed its interior. The remodeled bath house once again displays its original 1889 appearance, right down to the words "Basin water has made 90 percent of the cures of Eureka" written across the top.

When you're ready to leave the shopping district, turn left on Main and walk to the trolley depot. Here you'll catch a Red Route trolley back to the visitor center where your car is parked.

When you're ready to leave Eureka Springs, turn right on **Highway 62** after exiting the visitor center parking lot. Travel a short distance and turn left on **Highway 23 N** (Main St.), heading toward downtown. When you reach downtown, be sure to stay to the right where Spring St. runs into Main.

If you have time, there's one last stop on today's tour. **The Eureka Springs and North Arkansas (ES&NA) Railway** is just on the outskirts of town. (If you would rather head back to Branson, just continue driving north on Highway 23.)

The restored depot is a nostalgic trophy of the golden age of railroads, reminiscent of the time when passenger cars filled with vacationers rolled into town from far-off places. At the depot you can visit a gift shop with railroad memorabilia and a vintage railroad-car display. You can also ride the rails in a restored nineteenth century passenger car pulled by an authentic steam locomotive. The last one-hour excursion leaves at 4 P.M. Ticket prices are $9 for adults and $4.50 for children four to ten.

Flatiron III in Eureka Springs. *Photo courtesy of Flatiron Flats.*

The Way Back

After leaving the train depot, continue heading north on 23 for about 10 miles until it meets **Missouri 86**. Turn right on 86 to begin heading east. Missouri 86 will take you all the way back to **U.S. 65** (about 34 miles). It will, however, change directions a few times so watch the signs closely. Be sure to turn right when 86 joins with **Missouri 13**. The road will be marked 13/86 for about 3 miles until 86 takes off to the left. After turning left on 86, you'll be following the same route you did this morning. When you reach U.S. 65, turn left and head north for the 8-mile trip back to the U.S. 65 and Missouri 76 intersection.

To Plan a Return Visit

Eureka offers many other activities and attractions. To receive additional vacation information, contact the **Eureka Springs Chamber of Commerce**, (501) 253-8737, P.O. Box 551, Eureka Springs, Arkansas 72632.

Springfield, Missouri

Wilson's Creek
National Battlefield

Bass Pro Shops Outdoor
World

Wonders of Wildlife

Fantastic Caverns

Exotic Animal Paradise

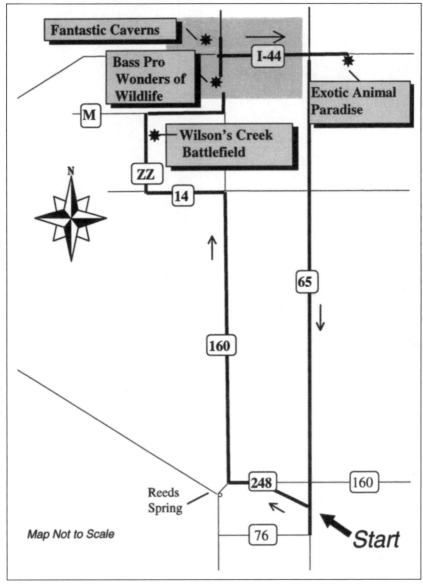

Fantastic Caverns

Bass Pro
Wonders of
Wildlife

I-44

Exotic Animal
Paradise

M

Wilson's Creek
Battlefield

ZZ

14

65

160

248

160

Reeds
Spring

Map Not to Scale

76

Start

Springfield, Missouri. *Approximate round-trip mileage: 150.*

Today's tour, a journey north to Springfield, Missouri, is a good trip for all ages at any time of the year. You'll stop first at a historic Civil War battlefield before traveling to Springfield to visit Bass Pro Shops Outdoor World—the most fascinating sporting-goods store in the country. Next to Bass Pro is the new in 2000 American National Fish and Wildlife Museum, also called Wonders of Wildlife. You'll also tour North America's only ride-through cave and one of the world's best drive-through wild-animal parks.

What to See and Do

- **Wilson's Creek National Battlefield Park**—This journey into history brings to life the bloody battle fought on this site in 1861.
- **Bass Pro Shops Outdoor World**—Besides sports equipment of all kinds at great prices, there's a museum, a four-story indoor waterfall, fish aquariums and even a McDonald's. Four million people visit Bass Pro each year.
- **Wonders of Wildlife—The American National Fish and Wildlife Museum**—In this $52 million project you'll come face to face with sharks, walk through a cave complete with live bats, and stroll over streams teeming with fish, beaver, and other wildlife. And there's lots of hands-on excitement for the kids.

- **Fantastic Caverns**—No need to worry about steps or tight places—this cave is large and level enough to ride a tram all the way through.
- **Exotic Animal Paradise**—America's largest animal park contains over three thousand wild animals. It's what all animal parks should be like.

Tips, Tactics & Timesavers!

- All attractions on this trip are open seven days a week, year-round.
- You might want to take a light jacket if you plan to visit Fantastic Caverns. The temperature is a constant and cool 58 degrees.
- If you'd like to plan a picnic, there's a quiet, shady picnic area at the caverns.

History of Springfield

In 1829 John Polk Campbell, from Tennessee, carved his initials in an ash tree to stake his claim here in the foothills of the Ozark Mountains. To promote the area, he donated 50 acres of land for a public square and gave cabins to settlers to encourage them to make Springfield their home. In 1833 the new community officially became Springfield, after (as legend has it) townsmen were offered a bribe of whiskey to vote for the name.

During our country's early years, the town square was the heart of the rural community. It was the place where people came to buy supplies, take care of government business and greet their neighbors. The Springfield square has witnessed much in its 160-year history. In the 1850s, after the city became a stop on the Butterfield-Overland Stage Line, a station was set up on its northeast corner. In those days, travelers heading west to California had to take a stagecoach from Springfield to Fort Smith, Arkansas. In Fort Smith they would board another coach on its way to San Francisco.

The square came under siege during the Battle of Springfield in 1863. When the hard-fought conflict was over, Union soldiers were forced to retreat, leaving the city for a time in the hands of the Confederates. Federal soldiers returned to take back the town, but fearing defeat, the Confederates had already withdrawn.

Springfield gained nationwide attention during the rough and rowdy Wild West era when in 1865 "Wild Bill" Hickok (one of the West's most flamboyant heroes) shot and killed a man on the square over a gambling debt. It was the first recorded Western-style gunfight in United States history.

In 1870 the St. Louis-San Francisco Railroad (the Frisco) chugged into town, bringing with it a new era of prosperity. Some fifty years later, the famed Route 66 (the first completely paved transcontinental highway in America) followed its legendary path through Springfield. Springfield is officially recognized as the birthplace of Route 66 because it was here on April 30, 1926, that the celebrated name was proposed. Signs of the historic route, nicknamed "Main Street USA," are still visible along Kearney, Glenstone, College and St. Louis streets, mostly in abandoned gas stations and long-closed tourist courts.

Today, Springfield (Missouri's third largest city) is thriving. The community has lots to offer its approximately 150,000 residents. The cost of living is well below the national average, and because of its proximity to Branson and the Tri-Lakes area, there's an abundance of entertainment and outdoor recreational opportunities.

Included on today's trip are some of the city's most notable attractions, but there's a lot more to see in Springfield. Other attractions include the **Missouri Sports Hall of Fame,** the **Dickerson Park Zoo,** the **Springfield Nature Center,** and the **Springfield History Museum.** If you would like to learn more about what the city has to offer, you can stop by the Convention & Visitors Bureau at 3315 E. Battlefield, or contact the Springfield Chamber of Commerce at (800) 678-8767.

How To Get There

From the **U.S. 65** and **Missouri 76** intersection, travel north on 65 for one mile to **Missouri 248/Shepherd of the Hills Expressway.** Exit to the right and travel to the stoplight, staying in the left lane. Turn left, crossing over U.S. 65, and begin traveling west. Missouri 248 will soon veer north, taking you on a scenic ride along the ridge tops. After about nine miles U.S. 160 will merge with Missouri 248 (continue straight at this intersection) and the route will be marked as both. Continue traveling on 160 (Missouri 248 will take off to the left, heading toward Reeds Spring) for about twenty-five miles to the town of Nixa.

In Nixa, the first major crossroad will be Missouri 14 (stay in the left lane as you approach the intersection). Turn left (west) and follow Missouri 14 for about 8.5 miles to **State Highway ZZ.** Turn right (north) on ZZ. In 1858 the Butterfield-Overland Stage Line carried mail and passengers along this historic route on its way south to Arkansas and then to points west.

It's about seven miles on ZZ to **Wilson's Creek National Battlefield Park.** Near the park you'll see a brown park sign on the right stating **Wilson's Creek Visitors Center.** Travel about a block past the sign, turn right, and drive another block to the park's entrance.

Wilson's Creek National Battlefield Park

Telephone: (417) 732-2662; Admission Range: No charge to tour the visitor center, but there is a $3 per person charge to tour the battlefield, or $5 per car.

The Battle of Wilson's Creek

The war between the United States of America (the Union) and 11 Southern states organized as The Confederate States of America (the Confederacy) lasted from 1861 to 1865. Although Missouri was officially a slave-holding state, most of its residents favored neutrality. Missouri's governor, Claiborne F. Jackson, however, sided with the South. When President Lincoln asked Jackson to supply troops, he refused and ordered state military units to seize a U.S. Arsenal near St. Louis.

The armory's commander, General Nathaniel Lyon, successfully defended the arsenal, and he and his troops pursued the Confederate military as they fled to Jefferson City, the state's capital. Jackson and his supporters were eventually forced to retreat to this area just south of Springfield.

By August 10, 1861, Jackson had amassed an enormous army of 12,000 men near Wilson's Creek. General Lyon,

Artillery demonstration at Wilson's Creek Battlefield. *Photo courtesy of Wilson's Creek National Battlefield Park.*

knowing he was outnumbered, having only 5,400 soldiers, planned a surprise attack, hoping to defeat the Confederates by catching them off guard. Initially his plan worked, and he was able to take the ridge now known as Bloody Hill. The Southern army continued to charge the hill, and possession seesawed back and forth several times. During one of the skirmishes General Lyon was killed. With their leader gone and their ammunition exhausted, the Union soldiers were forced to withdraw. The violent conflict had raged for more than five hours, and when it was over more than 1,700 Union and Confederate soldiers had been killed or wounded.

Although the Confederacy won the Battle of Wilson's Creek, they were unable to pursue the Federal soldiers north, and the southwest Missouri district remained under Union control. For the next three and a half years Missouri was ravaged by fierce fighting to determine whether it would stay in the Union or fall to the Confederacy. By the time the Confederates finally conceded, Missouri had witnessed so many battles and skirmishes that it ranked as the third most fought-over state in the nation.

The John Ray House, restored by the National Park Service, was used as a Southern field hospital during the Battle of Wilson's Creek.

The Visitor Center

On display in the visitor center are vintage photos and Civil War exhibits (don't miss the computer-controlled model showing troop movements and battle strategies). There's also an outstanding 12-minute slide show that brings to life the sights and sounds of the fierce struggle. Ask one of the staff for a showing—it's well worth the time.

The Battlefield Tour

If you decide to tour the battlefield, ask for a copy of the **Battlefield Tour Guide.** The 4.9-mile auto tour will lead you to eight historic points on the battlefield, and each stop features wayside exhibits. The only surviving structures associated with the battle are the Ray House and springhouse, built in 1852 (Site #2 on the tour guide). From 1858 until 1860 the Ray House also served as a flag stop on the Butterfield Overland Stage route.

If you enjoy walking, there are trails at Gibson's Mill, the Ray House, Price's Headquarters, Bloody Hill, and the historic overlook.

When ready to leave Wilson's Creek, return to Highway ZZ and turn right, heading north. If you would like to learn more about the Civil War west of the Mississippi, just a short way on ZZ is **General Sweeny's Museum of Civil War History** (look on the right for the American flag). The gallery features more than 5,000 antiques and artifacts. The museum is closed in December and January and is open only on weekends in November and February. *Admission is $3.50 for adults. Children twelve and under go free with a paying adult.*

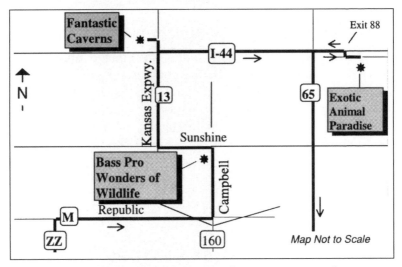

If you would rather not visit the museum at this time, continue heading north on ZZ for about a mile and a half to **Highway M.** Turn right on M (also known as **Republic Road**), heading east.

Your next stop is **Bass Pro Shops Outdoor World.** Stay on Republic Road for about seven miles until you reach **Campbell Street** (the first major street after crossing over the James River Freeway). Turn left (north) on Campbell and travel almost 3 miles to the stoplight at **Cherokee Street** (be sure to stay in the left lane). Turn left onto Cherokee and make an immediate right turn into the parking lot of Bass Pro. If the front lot is filled, there is additional parking farther down Cherokee Street

Bass Pro Shops® Outdoor World™

Telephone: (417) 887-7334 Web site: www.basspro.com

In addition to thousands of products for fishing, hunting, camping, golf and every other sport, there's an indoor showroom of boats; an indoor rifle, pistol and bow range; fresh- and salt-water aquariums, and a wildlife museum.

Touring Bass Pro Shops is like taking a walk in the great outdoors.

Even with all of the above, perhaps the most fascinating aspect of the sports center is its decor. Bass Pro is designed to bring the outdoors indoors. A focal point in the main showroom is a four-story limestone bluff with a cascading waterfall. Other outdoor-like features include a log cabin (the gift shop) and wooded walkways over pools filled with live fish.

To find your way around the huge 170,000-square-foot showroom, pick up a map at one of the checkout counters on your way in.

If you're ready for lunch, there are two choices right in Bass Pro. **Hemingway's Blue Water Cafe** (on the upper level) has a floor-to-ceiling, 30,000-gallon salt water aquarium overlooking the dining area. Seafood is the specialty, and a reasonably priced lunch buffet is featured daily. For something quicker, there's a **McDonald's** on the upper level near Hemingway's. If you're not ready for lunch, Fantastic Caverns (the next stop on your trip) has **The Smokehouse Restaurant** (open May 1 through October 31). The cavern

Bass Pro Shops Outdoor World.

also has a pretty picnic area, if you'd rather pick up sandwiches and eat outdoors.

Located within Bass Pro is a fish and wildlife museum featuring more than 750 animal mounts in settings simulated to look like natural habitats. *Admission range is $5.50 for adults, $2.50 for children five to seventeen, or $14.50 for the entire family.*

Money Saving Tip!

If you're planning to visit Exotic Animal World Paradise (and have at least three people in your party), Bass Pro has a coupon that's good for one free admission with the purchase of two tickets at the regular price. Ask at the checkout.

Wonders of Wildlife

The American National Fish and Wildlife Museum
Telephone: (877) 245-WILD
Web site: www.wondersofwildlife.org.
Admission Price: $11.25 adults; $9.75 seniors/students; $7.25 children four to twelve. Kids under four go free.

With more than 160 different live animal species, hunting and fishing displays, educational videos, and interactive computer-enhanced exhibits, this "much more than a museum" is a must see for anyone visiting the Ozarks. Besides viewing fish of all kinds (including a live shark in a 225,000-gallon saltwater aquarium), and a walk-though cave complete with bat sounds, you'll see otters, bobcats, snakes and more, all in delightfully realistic forest environments. Be sure to take your camera!

If these are the only attractions you wish to visit in Springfield, turn right on Sunshine Street (just north of Wonders of Wildlife). Sunshine will take you to U.S. 65. Turn right (south) on 65 to head back to Branson.

The next attraction is a ride-through tour of **Fantastic Caverns**, about eight miles north of Bass Pro. When ready to resume today's tour, head north on Campbell (turn left if exiting on Campbell) and travel in the left lane to the stoplight. Turn left (west) on **Sunshine Street**, and travel a little over a mile to **Kansas Expressway** (stay in the right lane as you approach the intersection). Turn right, heading north on the Expressway (also known as **Highway 13**). Continue traveling on 13 for about six and a half miles to **Fantastic Caverns Road** (after crossing Interstate 44, just follow the billboards to the cave). Stay in the center lane

Fantastic Caverns. *Photo courtesy of Fantastic Caverns.*

when you approach the turnoff because you'll be turning left, crossing the oncoming traffic lanes.

Fantastic Caverns

Telephone: (417) 833-2010; Admission Range: $14.95 for adults and $7.95 for children six to twelve. Children under five go free with a paying adult.

This is definitely the most convenient cave you'll ever tour. There's no need to worry about the walk being too strenuous or having to carry the little ones, because a tram takes you all the way through. Your tour guide will give some interesting highlights of the cave's history. For instance, during the 1920s the secluded hideaway was used as a speakeasy. A souvenir picture taken on your way in will be available for purchase when the tour is over.

If you would enjoy a short nature hike, there's a pretty half-mile trail beginning at the back of the parking area. Canyon Trail features limestone bluffs, wooden walkways, and a look at the Little Sac River.

The last stop on today's tour is **Exotic Animal Paradise.** When ready to leave Fantastic Caverns, turn left from the parking area and retrace your way back to Highway 13. Turn right on 13 and head south for a mile and a half to **Interstate 44** (stay in the left lane as you approach the intersection). Turn left, heading east on Interstate 44. The animal park is about fifteen miles from this point.

About midway, you'll come to U.S. 65. If you would rather return to Branson and not visit the animal park on today's tour, head south on U.S. 65.

To reach the animal park, leave the freeway at Strafford Exit #88. After exiting the highway, turn right at the stop sign and follow Highway 125 for one block to Highway OO. Turn left at OO and travel 3 miles to the park's entrance.

Exotic Animal Paradise

Telephone: (417) 859-2016; Admission Range: $10.99 for adults, $8.99 for seniors, and $6.99 for children three to eleven. Children two and under go free.

Have you ever visited an animal park and been disappointed because all the animals were nowhere to be seen? That won't happen here. The nine mile route will take you through woods and fields teeming with herds of buffalo, yak, ostrich, emu, elk, deer, antelope and hundreds of other species. Nearly three thousand wild animals roam free on 400 wooded acres. You'll make eye-to-eye contact with scores of inquisitive llamas, graceful gazelles, zebra, antelope, and deer. During certain times of the year you may even encounter a mild-mannered bear interested in what you're doing in his territory.

Be sure to allow at least two hours to visit the park. You'll want to have time to feed the animals and take pictures.

A side attraction, almost as much fun as seeing the animals, is feeding them (especially the baby deer). Food is available at the ticket booth, and you might want to buy a bag for each family member. Also available for purchase is an animal book to help identify the park's more unusual animals. Hold on to your admission receipt; you can exchange it for a free wildlife sketch at the park's gift shop.

Touring the Park

For safety reasons, it's recommended that you wind your car window down only about halfway. Many animals are very social and aren't a bit shy about reaching into your car for a handout.

The park's wilder animals include mountain lions, tigers, cougars and jaguars (these are behind bars), monkeys, buffalo, elk, big-horn sheep and Watusi cattle. The Watusi—a hardy breed of cattle from east central Africa—have horns that can measure as much as 6 feet between tips. The park has the largest breeding herd of Watusi cattle in America.

About two-thirds of the way through is the **Safari Center,** which has more animals, a petting zoo, paddleboats, go-karts (for an extra charge), gift shops, restrooms, a snack bar and an ice cream shop. Jeweled peacocks stroll the Safari Center's walkways, eager to display their glorious plumage. The main gift shop features unusual animal-related toys and gifts from around the world. (Don't forget to take your gate receipt to the gift shop for your free gift.) After leaving the Safari Center, the road will take you through the rest of the park and deliver you back to Highway OO.

Camel at Exotic Animal Paradise. *Photo courtesy of Exotic Animal Paradise*

The Way Back

Turn left and travel almost three miles back to **Highway 125**. Turn right on 125, cross over **Interstate 44**, and take the roadway to the left to head west toward Springfield. It's a seven-mile drive back to **U.S. 65**. To begin heading south on 65, stay in the right lane as you approach the 65/44 intersection. Travel under the freeway and follow the exit ramp off to the right. The ramp will circle uphill and put you into the southbound lane. It takes about forty-five minutes to travel the forty-five scenic miles back to Branson and Missouri 76.

Ozark, Missouri

Another town you might want to explore is Ozark, on U.S. 65 ten miles south of Springfield. Ozark is a flea-market mecca, and it would be easy to spend most of a day there. Visible from the freeway is a collection of several of the larger flea markets and antique shops. To find your way to other shops in town, ask any of the storeowners for a map and directory.

Ozarks Outdoors

Roaring River
State Park

Pea Ridge National
Military Park

War Eagle Mill

War Eagle Cavern

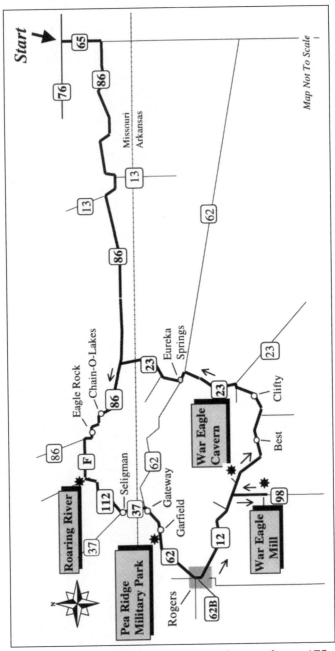

Ozarks Outdoors. *Approximate round-trip mileage: 175.*

Today's car tour is sure to be a family favorite. After breakfast in a country restaurant, you'll spend the morning visiting one of Missouri's most beautiful state parks. You'll then travel to Arkansas to the site of a historic Civil War battle. Lunch will be in a real working gristmill, and the last stop will include a narrated tour of a cave hidden deep in the Ozark hills. *See Tips, Tactics and Timesavers for restaurant details.*

What to See and Do

- **Roaring River State Park**—a beautiful spot in the wilderness with a pretty-as-a-picture trout stream, fish hatchery and scenic hiking trails.
- **Pea Ridge National Military Park**—a trip back in time to 1862, when Pea Ridge was the site of a fierce battle between the North and the South.
- **War Eagle Mill**—nostalgia at its best. The Mobil Travel Guide lists the mill's restaurant as "a place too special to be overlooked."
- **War Eagle Cavern**—featured are a spectacular natural entrance and an underground stream.

Tips, Tactics & Timesavers!

- The restaurant suggestion for breakfast is the **Tree Top Grille**, about a one-hour drive from Branson, featuring traditional country fare along with fresh-baked cinnamon rolls. Breakfast is served daily from 7 to 11 A.M., March 1 to October 31. Other times of the year it would be best to have breakfast before leaving Branson. Once you leave town you'll be traveling through rural areas where restaurants are few and far between.

- The suggested restaurant for lunch is at the **War Eagle Mill** in Arkansas. The country-style beans and cornbread are melt-in-your-mouth delicious, as are the sandwiches, made from the mill's own whole-grain breads. Lunch is served daily until 4 p.m. March through December. If traveling in January or February, there are other restaurants in nearby towns.

- If you can plan your trip in advance, mid-October is a wonderful time of year. The air is cool, the leaves have begun changing to their fall colors, and War Eagle Mill is hosting the Ozark Arts and Crafts Fair. For information and dates, call (501) 789-5398.

- Roaring River is a trout angler's dream, so if you have the necessary equipment you may want to take it along. The cool, clear, spring-fed stream is mighty tempting.

- Depending on your interests, you may not have time to see and do everything on today's trip. You might, for instance, prefer to spend more time than someone else would at the state park. If so, you could visit the park, travel to War Eagle Mill, and return to Branson, skipping the other attractions. It takes about an hour and a half to drive from the mill back to Branson. Like all the day trips, it's best to leave as early in the morning as possible.

How To Get There

From the **U.S. 65** and **Missouri 76** intersection, take U.S. 65 south for nine miles to **Missouri 86**. Turn right, heading west on 86 for about eleven miles. Missouri 86 will curve south and join with **Missouri 13**. At the Missouri 86/13 junction, turn right. The road is marked as both Missouri 86 and Missouri 13. After about 3 miles, Highway 86 will leave Highway 13. Turn left on 86, heading toward the towns of **Carr Lane**, **Chain-O-Lakes** and **Eagle Rock** (about twenty-two miles total).

Craggy rock formations, lazy cattle grazing on green meadows, and far-off views of distant mountain ranges will highlight your drive through Missouri's beautiful Mark Twain National Forest. If traveling in the fall of the year, you'll find roadside stands laden with baskets of just-picked apples, homemade cider, and jars of farm-fresh honey.

Just past Eagle Rock, you'll cross a small bridge spanning a narrow section of Roaring River. From the bridge, travel one mile to **Highway F**, turn left and follow it for five miles to the park.

Roaring River State Park

Telephone: (800) 334-6946; Season: From March 1 to October 31 you can visit the lodge, restaurant, nature center and hiking trails. From November through April the lodge and restaurant are closed, but the rest of the park is open. Winter fishing is restricted to Friday, Saturday and Sunday from the second Friday in November to the second Sunday in February; Admission: Free

Roaring River's rugged hillsides tell a fascinating geological story. Over eons the White River cut deep valleys into the vast plateau on which the reserve is located. Visible on the park's steep slopes are layers of sediment, such as shale, limestone, dolomite, and chert, which give evidence of the many changes in the earth's crust. The park is one of the few places in Missouri where you can easily see such a diversity of rock formations.

The scenic, spring-fed Roaring River began attracting white settlers in the 1830s. During those early years the spring provided power for a sawmill and gristmill—two services essential to the early pioneer. In 1928 a Kansas City businessman, Thomas Sayman, purchased 2,400 acres around the spring with the intention of turning it into a tourist attraction. He later abandoned the project and bequeathed the land to the state. Today the park is made up of 3,372 acres and is administered by the Missouri Department of Natural Resources' Division of Parks, Recreation and Historic Preservation.

As you near the park, rustic cabins (available for rent) will come into view. Immediately past these cabins, look to the left (just after passing a large brown park sign) for a road leading to Campground No. 3 and the Nature Center.

If you're having breakfast at the park, you may want to eat first and return later to visit the Nature Center. To locate the restaurant, continue traveling a short distance farther to Missouri 112. Turn left and travel uphill a short distance to the Roaring River Inn and Conference Center. Inside the Inn is the Tree Top Grille, featuring a great view of the park along with delicious fresh-baked pastries.

The Nature Center

At the Nature Center you'll find exhibits relating to native

Waterfall at Roaring River State Park.
Photo courtesy of Merle Rodgers, Dept. of
Natural Resources

birds, plants, animals and reptiles. There are more than six hundred species of plants in the park, many of which cannot be found in any other region of the state. A rare oak tree, the Ozark chinquapin, grows on many of the reserve's ridges.

One of the park's more scenic hiking trails, the **Devil's Kitchen Trail**, gives you a chance to see many of the park's special features. While at the Nature Center, ask for the brochure detailing the trail. The easy-to-follow booklet, filled with facts on geology, plant life and history, will turn the short hike into a real learning experience. The beginning of the trail is located across from **Roaring River Lodge**—the next stop on today's tour. After the hike, return the brochure to the Nature Center, or park store, for reuse.

To get to the lodge from the Nature Center, turn left on Highway F and travel to **Missouri 112**. Turn right, and right again at the stop sign on the other side of the bridge. The road will take you along the river, usually lined with anglers, and deliver you to the rustic, three-story C.C.C. Lodge where you can park. The Orvis Pro Shop on the lodge's third level has tackle, camping gear, fishing licenses and tags, hiking info, and bike rentals.

The Spring and Trout Hatchery

To find the spring and hatchery, follow the sidewalk to the left of the lodge. The spring, beginning in a deep, canyon-like gorge beneath the mountain, gushes more than twenty

Typical opening day of trout season at Roaring River State Park. *Photo courtesy of Merle Rodgers, Dept. of Natural Resources*

million gallons of water daily. In the spring of the year, or after heavy rains, the park affords an exceptional treat—a one-hundred-foot waterfall cascades from the cliff into the river. Look closely in the clear water in the deep pool and you might spot a lunker trout. The water gets its unusual blue-green color from minerals that filter into the river and refract light.

At the hatchery there are vending machines with food for the always-hungry trout in the raceways. Trout must reach 12 inches in length before they can be released into area streams, and it takes about 15 months for them to grow to the required length. If you're interested in a guided tour of the spring and hatchery, ask at the office, in the stone building on the far side of the raceways. The majority of the park's buildings were constructed in the 1930s by members of the Civilian Conservation Corps.

The park's shortest hiking trail takes off uphill between the spring and the hatchery. **Deer Leap Trail** will take you on a .2-mile trek (pretty much straight up) to an overlook above the waterfall for a striking view of the valley. The trail ends at the walkway leading back to the lodge.

Trout Fishing

As you can see by the avid anglers lining the river's banks, trout fishing is the park's premier activity. The stream, stocked daily during the season, provides plenty of first-class angling action. The clarity of the water makes spotting fish fairly easy, but trout are pretty crafty and it takes some real expertise to get them hooked.

To fish at the reserve, you must have a state fishing permit (except those 15 and younger, or Missouri residents 65 and older) and a daily trout tag purchased at the park. You need this daily tag even if you have a Missouri trout stamp, except in Zone 3, where the state license and trout stamp are adequate. The river is separated into three sections according to the type of bait that can be used in each. Zone 1 is posted as a "Flies and Artificial Lures" area. Zone 2 is "Flies Only," and in Zone 3 you can use "Artificial Lures and Natural Bait." The daily limit is five, and only a single rod may be used. For information, licenses and regulations, inquire at the park store.

Hiking Trails

The **Devil's Kitchen Trail** begins a short distance from the parking area in front of the lodge. Be sure to take your camera and the trail guide you picked up at the Nature Center. To find the trailhead, follow the road across the bridge to the picnic area. The trail begins behind the picnic tables.

The trail map will guide you to a number of stops, including Shelter Cave, a conifer forest, Trailside Spring Cave, and the rock formation for which the trail was named. Huge boulders, seemingly scattered by some giant's hand, make great backdrops for photos. In 1985 natural forces caused some of the boulders to fall, partly closing the front entrance to the area called the Devil's Kitchen.

You will be walking uphill for the first section of the trip, and downhill for the remainder. If you take your time and stop at all the stations, allow about an hour and a half to walk the trail, which will end at the road leading back to the parking area. There are several other trails in the park. If you would like a map of these trails, ask at the Nature Center or park store.

When ready to leave Roaring River, cross the bridge in front of the lodge and turn left, heading back to **Missouri 112**. Turn left onto 112 and begin heading south toward **Seligman**. There's a free observation tower you can visit about three-and-a-half miles from the park. If you would like to find it, look on the right for a park sign denoting

Sugar Camp Scenic Drive. Turn left onto the road directly across from the sign, and travel about two miles to where a gravel road takes off to the right, heading uphill. The road to the tower is pretty rough in spots, but the tower is worth finding. After climbing the killer stairs, you'll be rewarded with a superb view of the hills and valleys around Roaring River.

When ready to leave the tower, follow the gravel road back to the paved one, and turn left, retracing your way back to Missouri 112. Turn left on 112 and continue heading south.

From the observation-tower turnoff, you'll stay on Missouri 112 for about seven miles until it meets **Missouri 37** in Seligman. Turn left (south) on 37 and travel two miles to **Gateway**. (You'll cross the state line and enter Arkansas just before reaching Gateway.) When 37 meets **U.S. 62** in Gateway, turn right and follow 62 west toward **Rogers**.

About seven miles from Gateway, just past **Garfield**, is **Pea Ridge National Military Park** (the entrance is on the right). Your first stop is at the park's visitor center.

Pea Ridge National Military Park

Telephone: (501) 451-8122; Hours: 8 A.M. to 5 P.M.; Admission: There is no charge to tour the visitor center or see the film. To tour the battlefield the charge is $2 per adult or $4 per car. Web site: www.nps.gov/peri/

During the Civil War, control of Missouri was coveted by both the North and the South. In August 1861, at the Battle of Wilson's Creek near Springfield, the Confederates successfully stopped Union forces from claiming Missouri's southwestern district. By February 1862, however, Union Gen. Samuel R. Curtis had succeeded in pushing Confederate Gen. Sterling

Price and his army across the state line into Arkansas.

Near Fayetteville, Price joined forces with Gen. Ben McCulloch to retake the region. Gen. Earl Van Dorn took command of the 16,000-man force and headed north. Dug in on the bluffs overlooking Little Sugar Creek, not far from the small town of Pea Ridge, were Curtis' 10,500 Federals.

Van Dorn launched his attack on the morning of March 7 and captured the area around Elkhorn Tavern. On the morning of March 8 Curtis counterattacked. With his ammunition running low, Van Dorn was forced to withdraw. The Battle of Pea Ridge was the largest conflict west of the Mississippi and is considered the decisive battle in saving Missouri for the Union.

The Visitor Center

The sights, sounds and devastation of the battle are brought to life here in photographs, exhibits, and a twenty-eight-minute film titled *Thunder in the Ozarks*. The film is a perfect prelude to the battlefield tour. It can be shown at any time; just ask one of the staff when you're ready to view it.

There are ten miles of hiking trails through the park. The shortest one is a two-mile round trip hike from the visitor center to Elkhorn Tavern and back. Ask at the desk for details.

If you choose to pay to tour the battlefield, you will be given a free Battlefield Map and Guide. A more comprehensive tape-recorded tour is available in the bookstore for $5.

Touring the Battlefield

From the visitor center, follow the arrows painted on the pavement. For a short distance you'll be traveling on a section of the old historic Wire Road. It was given the name Wire (or Telegraph) Road in 1860, after a communication line was strung

Civil War scene from Ozarks Discovery IMAX film titled Ozarks: Legacy and Legend. *Photo courtesy of Ozarks Discovery IMAX.*

along it from St. Louis to Fort Smith, Arkansas. In the 1850s the Butterfield Overland Mail Company routed its stagecoaches along this road carrying mail and passengers to Fort Smith. (If you took the car tour to Springfield, you traveled a northern section of the Wire Road near Wilson's Creek Battlefield.)

The battlefield guide will take you to twelve key battle sites and describe the action that took place at each. The stops at the east overlook (No. 7) and Elkhorn Tavern (No. 9) have recorded messages. The original tavern was burned after the conflict, but the existing structure was rebuilt shortly after on the same foundation.

When you're ready to leave the park, turn right on U.S. 62, heading west to Rogers (about eight and a half miles). You are now on your way to have lunch at **War Eagle Mill**. Lunch is served daily until 4 P.M., and it's about a thirty-minute drive from this point. The mill is actually southeast of the battlefield, but because of Beaver Lake, you're having to head west, south and back east again to reach it. It's a pleasant drive through the lush Ozark hills.

Rogers and Bentonville

Rogers and the nearby town of Bentonville are not sleepy little country towns. Business here in northwest Arkansas is booming. Bentonville, a short distance to the west, is the world headquarters of Wal-Mart Inc. It's not included on today's trip because of time limits, but if you're ever traveling through town, be sure to find the **Wal-Mart Visitors' Center and Museum**. It's on the town square, in the variety store where Sam Walton, his wife Helen, and brother J.L. (Bud) Walton opened the first Walton's 5 & 10 in 1945.

In Rogers, when U.S. 62 meets **Business 62** (at the stoplight), turn left (south) on Business 62 (North Second St.) and drive one mile to **Highway 12**. Turn left on **Highway 12** (East Locust St.) and head east for twelve miles to **Highway 98**. When you reach Highway 98 (you'll see a sign on the right just before the turnoff that says War Eagle Mill), turn right and travel downhill a mile and a half to the mill.

War Eagle Mill

Telephone: (501) 789-5343; Admission: Free
Web site: www.wareaglemill.com

There have been four mills constructed on this site in the

War Eagle Mill. *Photo courtesy of Zoe Medlin Caywood, owner of War Eagle Mill.*

Sylvanus and Catherine Blackburn. *Photo courtesy of Zoe Medlin Caywood, owner of War Eagle Mill.*

last 160-plus years. The first was built in the 1830s by Sylvanus Blackburn. Sylvanus was just 21 when he left Tennessee, seeking to find his place in a new region. After discovering the wildlife-rich valley near War Eagle River, Blackburn constructed a two-story log cabin for himself and his wife, Catherine.

Sylvanus, together with other family members who came from Tennessee to join him, cleared the valley and founded a small community. By 1838, the town had a gristmill and sawmill, a blacksmith shop and a carpentry shop.

Over the years the Blackburn family became wealthy and influential in the region. Sylvanus and Catherine raised eight children—five boys and three girls. Both lived to be 79 and died within a few days of each other. After Catherine died on March 13, 1890, Sylvanus said he could not go on without her, and he passed away in his sleep five days later.

A severe flood destroyed the original mill in 1848, but it was quickly rebuilt. The Civil War was devastating to the Ozarks, and the War Eagle area was no exception. Two days before the Battle of Pea Ridge, the second mill was burned by the Confederates to keep it from being used by Union troops. In 1873, James Blackburn, a son of Sylvanus and Catherine, built the third mill. It stood until 1924, when it too was destroyed by fire.

Almost 50 years later the mill was raised again. In 1973, after careful research, Jewell and Leta Medlin and their daughter Zoe constructed an authentic reproduction of the one assembled 100 years earlier. It was the first new gristmill built in Arkansas in 90 years. Today, thanks to their efforts, we can all delight in this nostalgic memento of our country's heritage. The picturesque mill, the sound of the stone buhrs grinding and the hearty taste of whole-grain breads are reminiscent of life a century ago.

How War Eagle River Got Its Name

According to legend, the name was given in honor of War Eagle, a brave Indian who came to the area searching for the girl he loved. The Indian maiden, Se-quah-dee, had been abducted by a French trapper who also professed to love her. War Eagle found Se-quah-dee and the trapper along the banks of this river in the Ozarks. The young brave managed to slay the kidnapper, but was mortally wounded by another woodsman. Se-quah-dee, refusing to leave him, died by his side.

Although there is no written proof of this legend, old records show that the river was already named War Eagle when surveyors were sent to study the area shortly after the Louisiana Purchase in 1803.

Inside the Mill

The mill's first floor has a charming old-time general-store atmosphere. Behind the antique potbellied stove are shelves lined with jams, jellies, soup mixes, flour, cornmeal, baskets, and other country-style gift items. The milling operation takes place in back, and visitors are always welcome to watch the miller at work. Powered by an eighteen-foot undershot waterwheel, the mill grinds whole wheat, rye and buckwheat flour, cornmeal, grits, cereals, and other whole-grain mixes. If you would like to take a taste of the country back home, you can buy flour, cornmeal, and premeasured mixes for waffles, pancakes, and muffins.

If you need help baking that perfect loaf of bread, check out the *War Eagle Mill Wholegrain Cookbook*. It and six others are full of wonderful recipes. One includes low-fat recipes and another covers the use of whole grains in bread machines. All the books were written by Zoe Leta Medlin Caywood, one of the mill's owners. If you're interested in ordering products by mail, ask for a catalog—it has some great gift ideas.

Speaking of gifts, the mill's second floor houses the War Eagle Mercantile, filled with clothing and crafts. If you're hungry, though, you may want to eat first and shop later. The restaurant is one flight up.

The Bean Palace Restaurant

What makes this restaurant special, besides its picturesque

setting and homey country atmosphere, is the melt-in-your-mouth Ozark cooking. Ham and beans, the house specialty, is served in old-fashioned, blue-marbled graniteware bowls with thick squares of hearty cornbread on the side. Or you can order hickory-smoked ham or turkey sandwiches made with whole-grain breads. Tables are covered with red-checked tablecloths, and drinks are served in Mason jars. Complete your meal with whole-wheat carrot cake, blackberry cobbler or sugar-free apple pie. Lunch is in the $5 range. (Be sure to read the story of how the restaurant began on the back of the menu.)

The War Eagle Fair

Each year War Eagle Mill becomes the site of the Ozarks' No. 1 Arts and Crafts Fair. In mid-October, when the trees begin taking on the colors of fall, over five hundred exhibitors will attract more than 100,000 visitors to the four-day fair. Ask at the mill for details.

When ready to leave the mill, turn right from the parking area and retrace your way back to Highway 12. Turn right on 12, heading east. The road leading to **War Eagle Cavern** is about two miles farther (on the left). After turning, go slowly and watch carefully for signs. The cavern is open daily from mid-March until the first of November.

War Eagle Cavern

Telephone: (501) 789-2909; Hours: Daily 9 A.M. to 5 P.M.; Admission: Adults $7.95; children (six to twelve) $4.95. Web site: www.wareaglecavern.com

Stalagtites and columns in Indian Council Room in War Eagle Cavern. *Photo courtesy of War Eagle Cavern.*

A nature trail takes you to the cave, which was home to Indians hundreds of years before the white man settled in the region. The cavern's features include a spectacular entrance, an underground stream, unique onyx domes and an abundance of fossils. Safety-approved by the State of Arkansas, the cavern is well lighted, with wide walkways and no tight passages. Your guide will detail the cave's historical highlights during the 40-minute tour.

The Way Back

From the cavern, retrace your way back to Highway 12, turn left, and continue heading east for about thirteen and a half miles, traveling through the towns of **Best** and **Clifty** until you reach **Highway 23**. Turn left on Highway 23.

If you drive straight to Branson from this point, it will take approximately an hour and a half. The ride home features more picture-perfect views of sleepy hollows and a glimpse of historic **Eureka Springs**. *For a complete day trip to Eureka, see Chapter Seven.*

There are several attractions along the way back to Branson, and if you have time, you may want to include them on today's trip. One of these attractions is **Quigley's Castle,** a little less than 7 miles from the 12/23 junction. The road leading to it will take off to the left (the entrance is easy to miss, so you'll need to watch closely). The castle is closed Sundays and Thursdays.

Quigley's Castle

Telephone: (501) 253-8311; Hours: 8:30 A.M. to 5 P.M.; Season: April 1-October 31; Admission Range: Adults $5.50; children under fourteen go free

Quigley's Castle, known as "the Ozarks' strangest dwelling," is included as a "stage stop" on the petroleum industry's Ozark Mountain Trail. The curiously designed home (built in 1943) includes suspended rooms, floor-to-ceiling windows, and inside planting areas. The lively and eccentric Mrs. Quigley loved collecting, and incorporated in the walls of the home are her rock, arrowhead, and butterfly collections. The castle, now owned by the Quigleys' granddaughter, has been open to the public for over forty years.

Eureka Springs

After leaving Quigley's Castle, turn left on 23 and continue heading north for 4 miles to **Eureka Springs**. In Eureka, Highway 23 will meet **U.S. 62**. At this junction, turn left and follow 23/62 west for a short distance. Turn right on **Highway 23** (sign will direct you toward Beaver and Holiday Island) when it takes off from 62 and begins to head north to Eureka's downtown district. Be sure to stay to the right when you come to the fork in the road near the center of town.

There are several flea markets along Main Street (you will have to pay to park), and if you have the time you may want to check them out. At the end of Main, outside of town, is another point of interest. At Eureka's restored nineteenth century train depot, you can visit the historic station, a gift shop with train memorabilia, and a vintage railroad car display (all free of charge). You can also ride the **Eureka Springs and North Arkansas (ES&NA) Railway**. The last excursion leaves at 4 P.M. and the trip lasts about an hour. *Admission for adults is in the $8 range, and for children four-eleven, $4.*

After leaving the depot, continue traveling north on Highway 23 for about ten miles to **Missouri 86**. Turn right and stay on 86 (heading east) all the way back to U.S. 65 (about thirty-two miles). The road will change directions a few times, so watch the signs closely. Be sure to turn *right* when 86 joins with **Missouri 13** (toward Blue Eye). The road will be marked Missouri 86/13 for about three miles until 86 takes off to the left. (Watch closely for this turnoff. If you find yourself in Blue Eye, you missed the turn and will have to turn around.) Follow U.S. 86 to **U.S. 65**, turn left and head north for the eight-mile trip back to Branson and **Missouri 76**.

In the spring of the year flowering dogwood trees add beauty to Ozark hillsides.

Off the

Beaten Path

Big Cedar Lodge

Cosmic Cavern

**Berryville and
Kingston, Arkansas**

**Lost Valley
and Alum Cove
Hiking Trails**

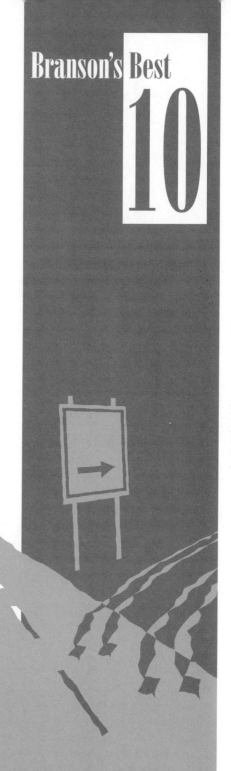

Branson's Best

10

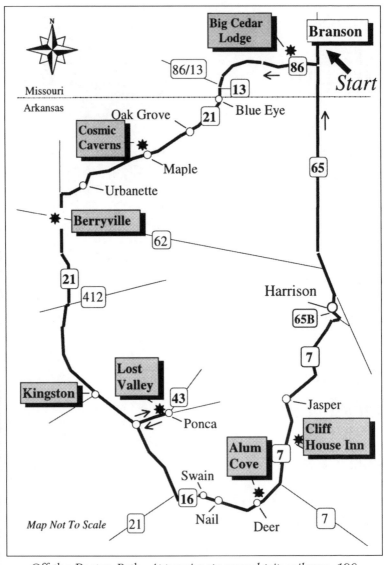

Off the Beaten Path. *Approximate round-trip mileage: 190.*

Today's car tour has a variety of activities. The day will begin with a gourmet breakfast at Big Cedar Lodge on Table Rock Lake. Then it's on to Arkansas to visit a cave, two historic towns and a museum or two. The noon meal will be in a quaint country town.

After lunch, you'll leave civilization behind and journey deep into the rugged wilderness to hike two scenic trails. The day will end with a relaxing dinner overlooking the "Grand Canyon of the Ozarks." *See Tips, Tactics and Timesavers for restaurant details*.

If there are more activities than you can complete in one day, take your time and choose those that interest you most. Even if you limit your trip to sightseeing from your car, it will be a trip to remember.

What to See and Do

- **Big Cedar Lodge**—stop for breakfast at one of the Branson area's finest resorts. *Midwest Living* includes Big Cedar among their "50 Top Vacation Destinations."

- **Cosmic Cavern**—an Ozark subterranean treasure.

- **Berryville, Arkansas**—off the tree-shaded square is the historic Carroll County courthouse, with a pioneer museum and heritage center. The museum is closed Saturdays and Sundays, and Mondays during the winter months.

- **Kingston, Arkansas**—a delightful small town in the middle of nowhere.
- **Lost Valley** and **Alum Cove**—two scenic hiking trails in the tranquil back country of the Buffalo National River.
- **Scenic Highway 7**—one of the top 10 scenic drives in the U.S.—"the best of the best scenic, fun-to-drive American highways," says *Car and Driver* magazine.
- **Cliff House Inn**—serves up delicious home cooking and a panoramic view of the "Grand Canyon of the Ozarks."

Tips, Tactics & Timesavers!

- To get the most out of your trip, pick a day when the weather is pleasant with good visibility. There are lots of outdoor activities and spectacular scenic views that go on for miles.
- It's better to take this trip Tuesday through Friday when all the restaurants and attractions are operating.
- **The Devil's Pool Restaurant,** suggested for breakfast, is at Big Cedar Lodge (about a ten-minute drive south of Branson). It's open seven days a week year-round. You have a choice of a full-service menu or an all-you-can-eat buffet from 7 to 11 A.M. The price for the buffet is $8.95 for adults and $6.95 for children four to twelve.

- **The Valley Café,** suggested for lunch, is in the remote town of Kinston, Arkansas. The café specializes in country-style plate lunches, sandwiches and hamburgers—all at very reasonable prices. The restaurant is closed Sundays.

- **The Cliff House Inn,** suggested for dinner, is on Scenic Highway 7, overlooking one of the Ozarks' deepest canyons. The restaurant is open until 8 P.M. Tuesdays through Saturdays, from Memorial Day to Labor Day (they close at 3 P.M. Sundays and Mondays). If you're traveling during another time of the year, you'll find other good restaurants along the way to and in the nearby town of Jasper.

- If you prefer dining in the great outdoors, there are shady picnic areas (with tables and restrooms) near both hiking trails.

- Be sure to take along a cooler filled with drinks. The hiking trails are in preserved areas with no vending facilities, and a cold drink on a hot day can be a lifesaver.

- It's best to fill your gas tank early in the trip or before leaving Berryville. You'll be traveling through rural country with little commercial activity and few gas stations. (A convenience market where you can buy gas and picnic supplies is mentioned near the beginning of the trip.)

- Tucked in a hillside at Lost Valley is a cave waiting to be explored. It's an undeveloped cave, though, and you need a pretty adventurous spirit to enter the pitch-dark cavern. If you think you might like to do some spelunking, take along a heavy-duty flashlight for each family member.

- This car tour has a really full schedule. You'll want to leave as early as you can and plan to return late.

How To Get There

From the **U.S. 65** and **Missouri 76** intersection, take U.S. 65 south for nine miles to **Missouri 86**. Turn right (west) on 86 and drive a half a mile to the entrance to **Big Cedar Lodge**. After turning right on **Devil's Pool Road**, travel down the hill about two miles to where a Big Cedar sign is located *above* a road taking off to the right. The narrow, one-way path will lead you through heavy woods and across flowing streams before it delivers you to the rustic four-story lodge called Valley View. To find the restaurant, follow the road to the left to the registration building and look for the signs directing you to Devil's Pool Restaurant.

Big Cedar Lodge

Telephone: (417) 335-2777; Web site: www.bigcedarlodge.com

Even if you aren't having breakfast here, it's worth the short trip down the hill just to see this beautiful resort over-looking Table Rock Lake. Outdoor sports of all kinds, and accommodations that include such comforts as Jacuzzis and fireplaces, make this one of the area's finest vacation spots. The resort, owned and operated by Bass Pro Shops, has amenities that include a fully equipped fitness center, a heated pool, bass fishing, trout fishing, hunting, boating, golf, and horseback riding. If you would like more information about accommodations or room rates, ask at the restaurant or at registration.

Devil's Pool Restaurant

Telephone: (417) 335-5141; Hours: Breakfast buffet from 7 A.M. to 11 A.M.; Season: Open all year

The Devil's Pool's woodsy hunting-lodge decor features rough-hewn beams, sturdy stone fireplaces, vintage fishing photos, a century-old mahogany bar, and lifelike animal trophies. Add a dynamite view of the lake, and you'll find yourself lingering over that last cup of coffee just to stay a little longer. The everything-you-could-want breakfast buffet features eggs, biscuits, gravy, bacon, sausage, ham, Belgian waffles, made-to-order omelets, fresh fruits, and pastries.

The building housing the restaurant was built by Julian "Jude" Simmons in the late 1920s to use as a weekend resort home. The exposed beam-and-log design is characteristic of the rustic hunting lodges of New York's Adirondack Mountains.

A pretty spot worth finding here at Big Cedar is **Devil's Pool Spring**. As you exit the restaurant, turn right and stroll to the suspended bridge off the side of the parking area (if you parked in the far lot, you may have already crossed the bridge on your way to the restaurant). The bridge spans a boulder- and rock-strewn gorge, affording a perfect photo spot. Before Table Rock Lake inundated the valley, a flowing spring bubbled up below the bridge. The spring was given the name Devil's Pool because early settlers thought it to be so deep that it could have gone all the way to the Devil's lair.

When ready to continue the day trip, follow the exit signs from the restaurant to the main road. Turn left and head back up the hill to Missouri 86. Turn right on 86 and continue traveling west, following 86 for 12 miles to **Missouri 13**.

> If you need gas or picnic supplies, Twin Island Market and Deli is about half a mile up the hill after you cross Table Rock Lake and Long Creek Arm Bridge.

At the 86/13 junction, continue straight to travel south on Missouri 13. *Don't turn right or you'll be on 86/13 heading west.* It's one mile to the town of Blue Eye, a small community straddling the state line. In the center of town just across the state line, Missouri 13 will become Arkansas **Highway 21**.

Continue traveling on 21 toward **Oak Grove** and **Maple**. Highway 21 features a myriad of postcard-pretty scenes with gentle rolling hills dotted with country farms and wildflowers. Northwest Arkansas is "Tyson Country" and many of the farmers in these parts raise chickens. As Tyson states, *"Here in Arkansas, the poultry industry is a lot more than just 'chicken feed.'"* One out of every 12 Arkansans is employed by the poultry industry—that's about 90,000 jobs and a $2 billion payroll. There are more than 2,500 contract growers statewide.

In Oak Grove, make a sharp right turn at the stop sign and travel about four miles to Maple and **Cosmic Cavern**. The cavern is located on the right, just after entering Maple's city limits.

Cosmic Cavern

Telephone: (870) 749-2298; Hours: seven days a week—9 A.M. to 5 P.M.; Season: Open year-round; Admission range: adults $10, children five to twelve $6, 4 and under go free

Cosmic Cavern features the area's largest subterranean lake, complete with trout, and the world's longest underground bridge. Your tour guide will take you to mysterious chambers featuring icicle-like stalactites, stalagmites, and

Cosmic Cavern. *Photo courtesy of Rodney Tennyson.*

delicate dripstone formations. The well-versed guides enjoy showing off the cavern and make the tour fun as well as educational. The tour lasts about an hour and covers one-third of a mile.

When ready to leave the cave, turn right and continue heading south on Highway 21 to and through **Urbanette**. From Urbanette, it's about five miles to the town of **Berryville**.

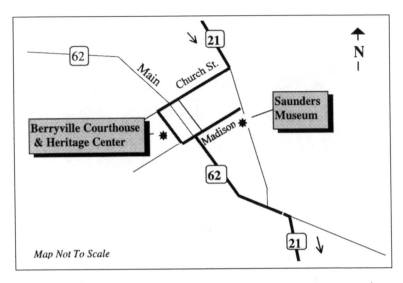

Map Not To Scale

Berryville, Arkansas (pop. 3,190)

In Berryville, turn right at **Church Street** (the second stop sign) and travel one block to the city's historic turn-of-the-century town square. Your first stop is the **Carroll County Heritage Center Museum**. To find it, follow Church Street to the stoplight at **U.S. 62** (also called **Main Street**). Cross Main and turn left at the first street. The museum is in the three-story red brick building in the middle of the block. If you enjoy viewing mementoes from the past, this may be the highlight of your trip.

Carroll County Heritage Museum

Telephone: (870) 423-6312; Hours: Mon.-Fri., 9 A.M. to 4 P.M.; Admission range: $2 for adults or $5 for the whole family

Berryville is the county seat of Carroll County, Arkansas. The region was settled in the early 19th century by homesteaders who came to the rough, wild Ozark mountains from Tennessee, Kentucky, Virginia and other southern Appalachian states. Many of the county's current residents are direct descendants of those hardy, rugged pioneers. The Heritage Center Museum is in the County Courthouse (built in 1880), which today is listed in the National Register of Historic Places.

The museum is a treasure trove of delightful old-time stuff. All three floors, including the stairways and halls, are crammed with hundreds of antique furnishings, vintage photographs, china, dolls, clothing, farm equipment and just about everything else used in everyday pioneer life. The majority of the museum's artifacts were donated by families living in the area, and the gallery's curators have used many of these items to simulate the way homes and businesses looked during our country's frontier days. There's a one-room schoolhouse, Grandma's parlor and kitchen, a barbershop, and an

The Carroll County Courthouse has been the focal point of the Berryville square since 1880. *Photo courtesy of Carroll County Heritage Center Museum.*

undertaker's office lined with pine boxes of various sizes. There's even a genuine moonshine still. The building's top floor (also filled with hundreds of old things) holds the court-house's original courtroom and judge's bench, set up as it was in the 19th century.

From the museum, you can walk to **Pioneer Memorial Park**, the town's original cemetery. The only preserved grave is that of Eliza (Polson) Berry, wife of the town's founder, Blackburn Henderson Berry. A granite marker lists the names of other early settlers buried in the graveyard. There's also a 150-year-old log cabin and a cell from the 1905 Carroll County Jail. (To get to the park, exit through the back door of the museum, cross the street and walk around to the far side of the library building.)

Around the Square

You can leisurely stroll to the tree-shaded square and relax on a park bench, or wander to the shops surrounding it. Today the square is used mostly for sitting, craft fairs and church sales, but during the Civil War it was put to use by Union troops as a rendezvous point and campground. In the early 1860s much of Berryville was set ablaze by both armies to keep the other side from gaining control of the town.

A shop you might enjoy visiting is **Berryville Drug**, where you can still get an old-fashioned ice cream soda or cone at an original 1950s soda fountain.

Another museum in town is the **Saunders Memorial Museum** on Madison Street. Madison runs beside Berryville Drug at the southeast end of the square. To find the museum, follow Madison east for one block. The gallery is on the right at the corner of Madison and Highway 21 (also called S. Springfield). Parking is in the rear. *(See map on page 200.)*

Saunders Memorial Museum

Telephone: (870) 423-2563; Hours: Mon.-Sat, 10:30 A.M. to 5 P.M.; Admission range: $3 range for adults and $1.50 for children under 13.

Col. C. Burton Saunders, an expert sharpshooter and avid collector of rare antiques, acquired his collection over a fifty-year period. The museum features a variety of weapons, silver, china, tapestries, vintage clothing, furniture, and trophies from around the world. You'll find Old West revolvers once owned by Billy the Kid, Jesse James, Sam Houston, and gangster Pretty Boy Floyd. Other exhibits include priceless dueling pistols, historic bowie knives, and an Arab sheik's tent.

When ready to leave Berryville, head east on Highway 62. If you're in the Saunders museum parking lot, return to the square and turn left (east) on 62. If you're at the courthouse, make a right turn on 62. *(See map on page 200.)*

Just down the road, **Highway 21** will join 62, and after a block it will take off to the right and begin heading south. Follow Highway 21 south for about eighteen miles (through Metalton) to **Highway 412**.

When 21 meets 412, turn right at the stop sign (you'll be on 412/21) and after traveling about three-tenths of a mile turn left on 21 as it leaves 412 heading south. (There's a small sign on the right directing you where to turn, but it's easy to miss. If you start heading toward the town of Marble, you've missed the turn.)

Kingston is about seven miles from the 412/21 intersection. The first stop sign in Kingston will be at the town square. Turn left and park at the Valley Cafe. If for some reason the restaurant is closed, there is a convenience store in town where you can pick up emergency provisions.

Kingston, Arkansas

You won't find any crowds or fast-moving traffic here; it's just the place to stop and take an unhurried stroll around a little country town. Until about 1960 Kingston served as a trading center for the surrounding rural community. As times changed, however, new roads bypassed the village, business went elsewhere, and Kingston stayed a small community where life is easy and slow-paced. The town's post office and bank still close for the noon hour.

The Valley Cafe

Telephone: (501) 665-2277; Hours: Monday through Thursday, 7 A.M. to 5 P.M.; Friday and Saturday, 7 A.M. to 9 P.M.

Since it was built in the 1930s, this building has housed a restaurant serving up country meals to travelers and nearby townsfolk. The hamburgers and fries are great, but if you're looking for some home-style cooking, be sure to check the lunch special.

Around the Square

You can see a remarkable piece of the past at the **Kingston Bank**, built in 1910. Through the window you can view the bank's original safe—as bright and shiny as if it were new. No one would guess that the state-of-the-art (at the time) vault was delivered to Kingston by wagon and team almost a century ago.

Two flea markets worth browsing are **Carlton Collectibles** and **Grandpa's**. Grandpa's proprietor knows lots of local history and has a library of books on the subject. If the owner is present, he will be happy to answer questions about the area.

Now you're on your way to **Lost Valley**, the first of the two hiking trails on today's trip. Lost Valley is in historic Boxley Valley. Boxley Valley (early settlers began establishing homes in the area in 1825) is registered in the National Register of Historic Places.

Follow Highway 21 out of Kingston, and head south for ten miles to **Highway 43**, where you'll make a sharp left turn (at the bottom of a very steep hill) heading toward the town of Ponca. Running parallel on the right, but a bit too far to see, is a narrow section of the Buffalo River.

After traveling 3.3 miles, look on the right for a brown sign indicating that you're near the Lost Valley turnoff. The park signs are designed to be unobtrusive, so you'll have to watch closely. (If you get to Ponca, you missed the turnoff.) Turn left at the first road after the sign and follow it to the parking area. Be sure to drive to the far end before parking the car. After the hike, you can make a quick trip to Ponca to see the river.

Lost Valley

Web site: www.ozarkmountains.org/lv.htm

The Lost Valley Trail can give you a real workout, or you can take it slow and easy. If you hike the entire trail, it's about three miles long. If you take the easy route, it's just two miles. This is the hike with the cave, so if you're going to explore it, be sure to take your flashlights when leaving the car. There are also lots of photo opportunities, so don't forget the camera.

The trailhead is a short distance from the parking area, and trail maps are available for a small charge. You might want to buy one to read about the area, but the trail is well marked and easy to follow without a map. Poison ivy, chiggers, ticks, snakes, and losing your way are all good reasons to make sure everyone stays on the trail.

The first mile is a level, easy walk along Clark Creek. Soaring bluffs, massive boulders, and a gently flowing mountain stream will lead you to Eden Waterfall, where you'll find a large bluff shelter once inhabited by Indians—picture-perfect settings for the camera buff! (Don't be tempted to drink the water, though, even if you're hot and thirsty. There's an organism sometimes found in these streams that can cause stomach upset.)

To keep the hike easy, retrace your way back to the car from this point. If you want to explore the cave, continue following the path up the hill.

Be forewarned: Just getting to the cave takes some athletic ability. Besides being steep, the half-mile trail becomes narrow, rocky, and difficult to navigate. The entrance to the cave is interesting, however, and the coolness of the cave's interior is welcome after the arduous climb. According to the hiking guide, if you go back about two hundred feet a passageway will lead to a large room and a thirty-five foot waterfall. We couldn't find the passage at the back, however, and crawling around in the dark, undeveloped cave is extremely difficult. But you may have better light and more endurance. When ready to leave the cave, follow the trail back to your car. About this time, you'll be glad you brought along those cold drinks.

From Lost Valley, retrace your way to **Highway 43** and turn left. It's just a mile to the small town of Ponca, where you'll get to see the river. Just before you get to town, follow the **Lake Access Road** off to the right.

The Buffalo National River

Web site: www.buffalonationalriver.com

The U.S. National Park Service, dedicated to protecting lands that are of historic, scenic, or scientific importance, declared the entire length of the Buffalo a national river in 1972. The only free-flowing river in the Ozarks, the Buffalo is wild, natural, and protected to keep it that way. You won't find any neon, theaters, or theme parks—rugged, unspoiled wilderness is the only attraction.

The river begins as a trickle in the Boston Mountains about sixteen miles southwest of Ponca. *(If you visited the Shepherd of the Hills Homestead, you saw these mountains from the top of Inspiration Tower.)* It then takes a 135-mile journey east through the Ozarks before emptying into the White River south of Mountain Home near Buffalo City. Due to its extensive length, the park is divided into three districts, each one having its own individual characteristics.

Because no roads parallel the river, and there are few easily accessed overlooks, the best way to see the park is by trail or by canoe. Today you are visiting the upper or west end of the river—the largest and most rugged of all the districts. Canoeing enthusiasts particularly like this section of the river in the spring and winter, after heavy rains turn the usually quiet stream into a churning stretch of whitewater excitement (other times of the year, the water level here may be too low to float).

"A run up on Boxley" is how locals refer to this stretch of the river. In the springtime or after heavy rains, hairpin turns and waves as high as two and a half feet will put your canoeing skills to the test. Some outfitters offer rafting trips as well as canoe trips. If you're interested in a float trip, stop at the **Buffalo Outdoor Center** (BOC), (800) 221-5514, in Ponca for information. The BOC can provide everything you need for a single day's trip or longer. While there, you can pick up a map of the **Buffalo National River Park**.

Floaters often catch a glimpse of the elk that make their home in the Ponca area. An estimated 450 animals have grown from a successful restocking program that brought 112 elk in from Colorado and Nebraska in the early 1980s. Black bear are at home here, too, although these shy creatures are not often seen.

Other locations along the Buffalo you may want to visit on future day trips are the **Pruitt Ranger Station** (east of Ponca), the **Tyler Bend** area (the center district) and **Buffalo Point** (at the eastern end). The Tyler Bend station has a visitor center, campgrounds, picnic facilities, and hiking trails. The visitor center features geological exhibits and an auditorium where a variety of programs about the park are presented. This middle section of the Buffalo offers lots of privacy, hiking trails, and quiet, gentle floats during both spring and summer months.

Suitable for floating year-round is the Buffalo Point district, at the far eastern end of the river. This is the most popular district along the Buffalo, because it offers such amenities as full hook-ups, a restaurant, and cabins. Near the Buffalo Point Station, almost hidden from the world, are the ghostly remains of Rush, a once prosperous zinc-mining community. Deep in the wooded hollow, lonely skeletons of old town buildings stand guard over the memory of the turn-of-the-century mining town. During the summer, tours are offered at the Buffalo Point Information Station.

After heavy rains, the Buffalo often turns a unique shade of blue-green. Here's the explanation for this change, as given in *Currents*—the Buffalo River Visitors Guide:

"Weathered microscopic clay particles from shale outcrops are washed into the river during rains. Small particles of silt and clay are suspended in the water while the river level is high and the water flows rapidly. As the river level drops after a heavy rain, large silt particles, which make the river muddy, are carried downstream or settle to the river bottom.

"Unlike silt, the fine, light clay particles remain suspended in the water for weeks. These suspended particles interfere with the passage of light. Light bounces among the suspended particles and separates into the colors of a rainbow. Of these colors, only blue and green are reflected, giving the river its turquoise color.

If you would like to find out more about the park, hiking trails or float trips, contact: Superintendent, Buffalo National River, P.O. Box 1173, Harrison, Arkansas 72602, or call (870) 741-5443.

Bluffs towering 500 feet or more are common on the Buffalo National River. *Photo courtesy of Buffalo Outdoor Center.*

'If you need supplies, there's a small general store in Ponca just up the hill from the river. If not, you're on your way to **Alum Cove** for another short hike. When ready to leave Ponca, follow **Highway 43** back to **Highway 21**. Turn left and head south on 21 for eleven miles to **Highway 16**. Turn left (east) on 16, heading toward the towns of **Swain**, **Nail** and **Deer**. It's about eleven miles to Deer from Highway 16.

About a mile past Deer, begin looking on the right for a sign indicating you're near Alum Cove. Make a left turn on **Forest Road 1206** and travel three miles to **1206a**. Turn right and follow the road to the parking area.

Alum Cove

On the far side of the picnic area is a large brown sign displaying a giant map of the Alum Cove trail. Not far from the trail's beginning, you'll see a spot where the trail forks. From this point, if you take the trail to the left, you'll head directly to the trail's more scenic features—a 130-foot natural arch and a series of cave-like rooms weathered out of massive rock bluffs. When you get to the end of the bluffs and start into the woods, you may want to turn around and hike back the same way you came, skipping the rest of the trail (there are no other bluffs once you begin going into the forest).

The hike up the hill is strenuous, so take your time and rest along the way. Nearby benches provide the perfect place to relax and reflect on the undisturbed and tranquil forest that surrounds you.

When ready to leave Alum Cove, retrace your way back Forest Road 1206a to 1206. Turn left and travel back to Highway 16. Make a left on 16 and drive about one mile to

Highway 7. Turn left on Highway 7 and begin heading north. It's about eight miles to the **Cliff House Inn** from this point.

Scenic Highway 7

Scenic Highway 7 is a five-star attraction brought to you by Mother Nature and Father Time. Stunning Ozark vistas at every turn are the specialty of this unforgettable stretch of roadway riding the ridgetop above Big Creek Valley. Your first glimpse of the longest, deepest canyon in the Ozarks will take your breath away, and every bend in the road will bring new scenic views.

Cliff House Inn and Restaurant

Telephone: (870) 446-2292; Season: March 17 to November 1; Hours: From March 17 to May 29 the hours are 8 A.M. to 3 P.M. daily. From Memorial Day (May 30) to Labor Day (first Monday in September) hours are 8 A.M. to 3 P.M. Sunday and Monday, and 8 A.M. to 8 P.M. the rest of the week. After Labor Day the 8 A.M. to 3 P.M. daily schedule resumes.

The Cliff House Inn has a lot to offer—great home cooking (the fresh-made rolls and desserts are wonderful), reasonable prices, and one of the best views in the Ozarks. It's the perfect ending to a relaxing day of hiking and sightseeing.

The Way Back

When ready to leave the inn, turn right and continue

heading north on Highway 7. If the Cliff House Inn was closed, you won't have to travel far to find the **Mockingbird Motel and Restaurant**. Open year-round, they also feature homemade pies and country cooking.

Next to the Mockingbird Restaurant is **Sloan's Mountain Antiques and Flea Market**. If you have the time, stop and browse for an old-time treasure or to take a funny photo— hillbilly style!

There are more restaurants in **Jasper,** about five miles farther. Jasper, another historic Ozark town established in 1840, is a stopping-off place for many visitors exploring the Buffalo River area. If you would like vacation information for a future trip, contact the Jasper/Newton County Chamber of Commerce, P.O. Box 250, Jasper, Arkansas 72641, or call (870) 446-2455.

Highway 7 will take you through Jasper and on to **Harrison** (about 18 curvy, scenic miles). If you have the time and the energy, you may want to visit **Mystic Caverns**, (870) 743-1739, about 8 miles south of Harrison. There are two caves here, with each presenting varied underground trea- sures. It takes about an hour to visit both caves, and the last tour begins at 3:45 p.m. *Admission range is $8.95 for adults and $4.95 for children 5-12. Children 4 and under go free.*

In Harrison, Highway 7 will make a jog to the right before it merges with **U.S. 65B**. Turn left (leaving Highway 7) on U.S. 65B and follow it through historic downtown Harrison. (If you miss the turn, Highway 7 will connect with U.S. 65 a little far- ther down, and you should make a left turn at this junction.) Business 65 will merge with **U.S. 65** (stay straight at this inter- section), and continue heading north toward Branson. It's an easy, scenic 35-mile drive back to Branson and Missouri 76.

Points North

George Washington Carver Monument

Precious Moments Chapel Center

Carthage, Missouri

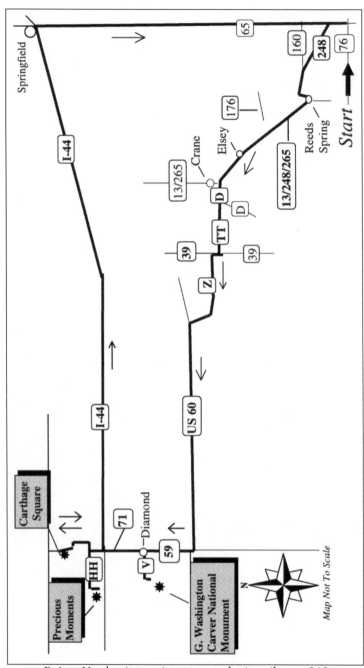

Points North. *Approximate round-trip mileage: 213*

Today's trip will take you on a two-hour journey north to Carthage, Missouri. Along the way you'll make a stop at the George Washington Carver National Monument before traveling to Precious Moments in Carthage. After touring Precious Moments, you'll head to flower-filled Courthouse Square.

What to See and Do

- **George Washington Carver National Monument—** a museum and nature trail commemorating the life of a great educator and outstanding innovator in the agricultural sciences.
- **Precious Moments Chapel Center**—an inspiring memorial designed by the creator of Precious Moments figurines, Samuel J. Butcher.
- **Carthage, Missouri**—site of the first full-scale land battle of the Civil War. Featured are a Civil War Museum, the historic Jasper County Courthouse and century-old Victorian homes.

Tips, Tactics & Timesavers!

- Precious Moments Chapel and the George Washington Carver National Monument are open seven days a week, (except for major holidays), year-round. The courthouse and visitor center in Carthage are closed on weekends.

- Because of the two-hour drive, it's best to have a quick breakfast and leave as early in the day as possible.
- If you would like a free Missouri map, stop along the way at the Branson/Lakes Area Chamber of Commerce and Visitor Center.

How To Get There

From the **U.S. 65** and **Missouri 76** intersection, take 65 north for one mile to **Missouri 248** (staying in the right lane as you approach the intersection). Exit right, travel to the stoplight and turn left (west), crossing over U.S. 65. The **Branson/Lakes Area Chamber of Commerce and Visitor Center** is immediately on the left. If you stop to pick up a map, turn left when leaving the visitor center.

Missouri 248 is a curvy mountain road that will surprise you with spectacular views of lush timberlands, deep valleys and distant mountain ranges. Later in the trip the hills will level out, presenting a more rolling countryside. Farther north the land becomes fairly flat, and neatly spaced rows of corn and soybeans lead the way to tall silos, red barns and white-washed farmhouses.

About nine miles from Branson, Missouri 248 joins **U.S. 160**. At this junction, drive straight to continue traveling west on 248/160 (the route will be marked as both). After traveling about five miles, you'll leave 160 and follow Missouri 248 when it takes off to the left toward **Reeds Spring**. Follow 248 for two miles to the stop sign in Reeds Spring. Turn right and head north on **Missouri 13** (also marked as 248 and 265).

You'll travel on Missouri 13 for about eight miles until it intersects with Missouri 176 near Galena. Just before reaching

176, you'll come to Galena's historic Y Bridge. Spanning the James River, the Y Bridge, built in 1927, is listed on the National Register of Historic Places. You might want to stop and take a minute to read the historic marker and stroll across the bridge and up the hill to view the Stone County Courthouse (also on the National Register) in the town's square.

The tiny town of Galena has a rather gruesome legacy. Several historians have cited it as having been the site of the nation's last large-scale public execution. In 1937 Roscoe Jackson, a confessed murderer, was hanged in the square before an audience of more than four hundred people. Many remember the scene as having a carnival-like atmosphere. The next year, the state ordered that all executions be carried out in the gas chamber in Jefferson City.

When ready to leave the Y Bridge, turn left and travel a short distance to Missouri 176. At this intersection, turn left and follow Missouri 13 for about nine miles through **Elsey** and toward **Crane**.

Close to Crane (just inside the city limits), watch closely for **Highway D**. (If you go over the railroad tracks in town, you missed your turnoff.) Turn left on D, heading west toward Wheelerville. After turning left on Highway D, turn left again (after about a car length), following the road signs (you'll be traveling on a side road paralleling Missouri 13). After one block, turn right (by the Stone County National Bank) and begin heading west. After almost two miles, **Highway TT**

If you're short on time, or would rather travel directly to Precious Moments and not visit the Carver National Monument, stay on Missouri 39 until you reach Interstate 44 in Mount Vernon. Head west on I-44 toward Joplin. Take the U.S. 71 exit at Carthage and follow 71 to Highway HH. Turn left on HH and follow the signs to Precious Moments.

will split off from D. Veer to the right on TT, following it for seven miles (through **Reavisville**) to **Missouri 39**. Turn right (north) at the stop sign and travel one mile to **Highway Z**.

To find the **George Washington Carver Monument**, turn left (west) on Highway Z and travel about 8½ miles to where Z meets **U.S. 60**. Turn left (toward Monett) on 60 (continuing west) and drive about 26 miles to **Missouri Highway 59**. Turn right on 59, heading north for 6 miles to **Highway V** in the town of **Diamond**. Turn left on V, travel about 2 miles, and look for a sign directing you to turn left on **Carver Road.** It's less than a mile to the park's entrance.

George Washington Carver National Monument

Telephone: (417) 325-4151; Hours: 7 days a week, 9 A.M. to 5 P.M.; Season: Open year-round; Admission: Free

George Washington Carver (1864-1943) was a famous African-American agronomist (agronomy is a branch of agriculture dealing with field-crop production and soil management). He was also a botanist, "cook stove chemist," gifted artist and respected educator.

Carver, born a slave here in Diamond, lived on the farm until he was about ten years old. He eventually moved to Kansas, worked his way through high school, and went to the Iowa State College of Agriculture. In 1896 he became director of agricultural research at Tuskegee Institute in Alabama. His goal was to help improve life for "the man farthest down."

Finding that single-crop cotton cultivation had exhausted the once fertile Southern farmlands, Carver encouraged farmers to plant nitrogen-producing legumes (like peanuts and soybeans) and high-yield products such as sweet potatoes. His breakthrough research with hybrids and various types of fertilizer caused spectacular results in growing larger and healthier plants.

George Washington Carver. *Photo courtesy of George Washington Carver National Monument.*

Many farmers took Carver's advice, but found no ready markets for their now abundant crops. Faced with this new dilemma, Carver began an exhaustive series of experiments that resulted in more than 300 byproducts of peanuts, sweet potatoes and soybeans. He also perfected a new type of cotton known as Carver's hybrid. His discoveries of the commercial possibilities of these products virtually changed the economy of the South.

Carver, a charismatic speaker, had a gentle, compelling manner. Young people were especially drawn to him—both black and white—and through his encouragement and example many students were motivated to continue their education.

Carver died in 1943, three years after donating his life's savings for the establishment of the George Washington

Carver Foundation at Tuskegee for research in natural science. He was elected to the Hall of Fame for Great Americans in 1973.

Don't miss the 28-minute film about Carver's life titled *Man of Vision*. Ask at the desk for the time of the next showing.

The Nature Trail

The trail will take you on a pretty walk through thick woods, over footbridges and along a flowing spring-fed stream to the site where Carver was born, a sculpture of George as a boy, a house built by his father, Moses, in 1881, and the Carver Family Cemetery. A guide that can be purchased for a small charge highlights the trail's points of interest.

Carver's presence can still be felt here in the place of his birth, along the shady path where he played as a boy in the beauty of the forest that surrounds it. His profound religious faith and deep love of nature prompted Carver to write ". . . Never since have I been without this consciousness of the Creator speaking to me through flowers, rocks, animals, plants, and all other aspects of His creation."

When ready to continue the day trip, turn left when exiting the park and travel back to Highway V. Turn right to retrace your way back to Missouri 59. Turn left on Missouri 59, heading north. You're now on your way to **Precious Moments** in nearby **Carthage**.

After about six miles, 59 will cross under Interstate 44 and change to Highway 71. Follow 71 about 4 miles farther to Carthage **Exit HH**. Exit the highway to the right, turn left on HH, and follow the signs to Precious Moments.

Samuel J. Butcher. *Photo courtesy of Precious Moments.*

Precious Moments Chapel Center

Telephone: (800) 445-2220; Season: Open year-round (closed Thanksgiving Day, Christmas Day, and New Year's Day); Admission prices: Chapel tour-Free; Fountain of Angels-$9; Wedding Island-$8; Art Museum-$8; Day Pass-$10 ($9 seniors), $3 for children four to sixteen. The Day Pass includes all the attractions at Precious Moments.
Web site: www.preciousmoments.com

Precious Moments is the realization of a dream conceived by one of America's most beloved artists, **Samuel J. Butcher.** He explains, "The Chapel is my gift of thanksgiving to the Lord for all that He has given me. It's also my gift to all the people who appreciate Precious Moments so that they might come and see the expression of my love for the Lord." Butcher chose to build the tribute to his faith in Carthage, where he lives and works.

Besides the Chapel, the Center's original and only free attraction, there are three other attractions at Precious

Moments. All added in the last few years, they are: The Fountain of Angels (a spectacular music, water, and light show); The Art Museum (tour of the charmingly decorated home where Butcher once lived); and Wedding Island (two furnished Victorian homes and a church). As shown in the admission price list, the Day Pass is definitely the best buy. Descriptions of all attractions are given later in the chapter.

The Visitor Center

The delightful visitor center is an attraction in itself. The thousands of twinkling lights covering the ceiling and outlining the European-style storefronts create a fairyland effect complemented by animated showcases of Precious Moments characters. To the right of the entrance is the counter where you can make reservations for the next Chapel tour and purchase tickets for other attractions. Be sure to ask when the Fountain of Angels shows are scheduled, and catch the earliest one. Two different shows are presented and you might want to see both.

Musical entertainment is also presented in the visitor center. The show, featuring gospel, bluegrass, and country music, is performed daily during the busy season, on the hour (excluding the noon hour), beginning at 11 A.M. Check at the desk, as times are subject to change.

If you're ready for lunch, **Royal Delights**, located in the visitor center, features affordable deli-style sandwiches, snacks, and desserts. And if you have time before the Chapel tour or Fountain of Angels show, stop in at the gift shop and check out the "Chapel Exclusives," special items that can be purchased only here at Precious Moments headquarters.

The Chapel

The exquisite five-thousand-square-foot-chapel contains fifty-four inspiring murals and fifteen stained-glass windows

Each of Precious Moments Chapel's fifty-four murals depicts one of Butcher's favorite Bible stories. *Photo courtesy of Precious Moments.*

designed and hand-leaded by Butcher and his family. The largest mural is on the ceiling. Spanning 2,600 square feet, it portrays cherubs floating overhead to create the illusion of Heaven. Other murals, painted in deep, rich Renaissance tones, depict scenes from the artist's favorite Bible stories, incorporating his charming trademark characters. From the chapel's terrace you can see **Grandpa's Island,** complete with a child-size castle designed by Butcher for his grandchildren.

Another not-to-miss attraction near the Chapel is the **Art Gallery**. The gallery showcases the Enesco product display, illustrating all phases of figurine production. Also exhibited is an array of art and memorabilia collected by Butcher during his career, and a complete collection of Precious Moments figurines dating back to their original 1978 release date.

The Fountain of Angels

The fastest way to get to where the show is presented is to return to your car and drive across the street to the parking lot directly across from the visitor center. You can't miss the entrance to the huge five-hundred-seat, air-conditioned theater.

With approximately 252 bronze sculptures, including 120 bronze angels, some weighing as much as one thousand pounds apiece, the Fountain of Angels is a glorious sight to behold. It took Butcher five years to design the fountain, complete with a visually stunning fifteen-minute water, light, and video presentation. The inspiring musical score was created with the help of London's Philharmonic Orchestra. There's also a thirty-minute preshow presented by a trio of talented gospel singers. It's hard to think of anyone not enjoying this one-of-a-kind attraction.

The Art Museum Tour

The only way to get to the Art Museum is by bus (the

loading area is in front of the visitor center). Housed in the residence that Butcher renovated and lived in while painting the Chapel, the Art Museum showcases furnishings and art pieces he acquired on his travels around the world. The brochure you received when boarding the bus has a listing of special items in each exquisitely decorated room. You can spend as much time as you like on the self-guided tour before boarding a bus back to the visitor center.

The Victorian Wedding Island

You might want to catch this attraction on your way out, when you're ready to leave the Precious Moments Chapel Center. After returning to your car, turn left after exiting the parking area and drive one block to the entrance to Cubby Bear's RV Park. Turn right and follow the road until it ends in a parking lot by a large barn. A bus will be along shortly to take you to the Island.

The idea for Wedding Island came about after a Methodist congregation in Stotts City, Missouri, offered their deteriorating church building to Butcher. After accepting, Butcher decided to use it as the centerpiece of a magical place to hold fairytale-like weddings and receptions. Two homes are also on the island, the **Victorian Mansion** and the **Bride's House**. Be sure to take time to read the Wedding Island brochure as you tour the church and homes.

When ready to leave Precious Moments, follow Chapel Road back to Highway HH. Turn right on HH and follow it (you'll cross over the freeway) to **Missouri 571** (about one mile). Turn left on 571, heading north. After about half a mile, 571 will veer off to the left. Continue driving straight at this intersection to begin traveling on **Grand Avenue**. The north end of Grand is lined with Victorian-style homes built during the city's golden days. The oldest home (at 1163 Grand) is the

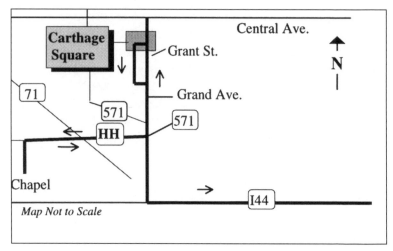

Map Not to Scale

Spencer House, constructed in 1870. (More historic homes are located on Main Street, one block to the west.)

When Grand ends at **Eleventh Street**, make a jog to the left and then right to begin traveling on **Grant Street.** As you near the downtown square, you'll see the **Jasper County Courthouse,** towering majestically above the treetops.

Carthage, Missouri

Carthage, founded in 1842, has the distinction of being the site of the first major land battle of the Civil War. The battle, fought on July 5, 1861, was written up in the New York Times of July 14, 1861, as "the first serious conflict between the U.S. troops and the rebels."

Early in July of that year, pro-Southern Missouri Governor Claiborne F. Jackson, seeking to take 6,000 members of the Missouri State Guard south to join the Confederacy, was confronted here in Carthage by one thousand Union volunteers commanded by Col. Franz Sigel. After a fierce battle, the outnumbered Union soldiers were forced to retreat, and southwest Missouri stayed under Confederate control. In 1862, however, a decisive Union victory at Pea Ridge, Arkansas, saved Missouri for the Union. *To visit or learn more about Pea Ridge Military Park, see Chapter Nine.*

Although much of Carthage was destroyed during the war, the town fought hard to recover. Surrounding lands contained rich deposits of lead, zinc, and marble, and much of the community's wealth came from mining these natural resources. At the end of the nineteenth century, Carthage had more millionaires per capita than any other city in the United States. It was during this time of prosperity that the city's wealthy businessmen were able to build the gracious and elegant Victorian homes seen throughout the Carthage historic district.

Where To Park

A convenient place to park is on Third Street, near the **Carthage Chamber of Commerce Visitor Center** Telephone: (417) 358-2373. From there you can stroll to the courthouse and then around the corner to visit the Civil War Museum.

To find the Visitor Center, drive past the courthouse and turn left on **Third Street.** The Visitor Center is on the right near the end of the block. At the Visitor Center you can pick up a town map and a brochure detailing the city's lovely old Victorian homes. Also available (for a small rental fee) is a cassette tape that narrates an easy-to-follow tour of the historic residential district.

One of the town's elegant Victorian mansions, the Queen Anne, can no longer be seen in Carthage. It was moved to Eureka Springs, Arkansas, in 1984. It took thirty-seven lowboy trailers, three storage vans, and more than $500,000 to move and restore the home in Eureka Springs. *For information on Eureka and the Queen Anne Mansion, see the Index or Chapter Seven.*

Around the square are many wonderful flea markets and hometown shops worth browsing. And when you're ready to give your feet a rest, check out **Carthage Deli and Ice Cream**, a fun shop with a 1950s theme. Half of an antique car holds seats for sipping double-dip ice cream sodas and old-fashioned shakes.

Historic Jasper County Courthouse in Carthage, Missouri. *Photo courtesy of Carthage Chamber of Commerce.*

Jasper County Courthouse

Hours: Mon.-Fri., 9 A.M. to 4:30 P.M.

M.A. Orlopp, of New Orleans, designed the Jasper County Courthouse early in the 1890s at a projected cost of $91,600. Extra funds were needed, however, when the city decided to dig until a limestone base was reached to assure that the new courthouse would have a solid rock foundation. In 1894, when time came to lay the cornerstone, 15,000 people lined the streets to celebrate the occasion with a parade and fireworks. The courthouse, along with the buildings around the square, is listed on the National Register of Historic Places. listed on the National Register of Historic Places.

Inside, you can view several memorabilia exhibits, a vintage elevator installed in 1917, and a mural painted by local artist **Lowell Davis**. The painting, "Forged in Fire," portrays the history of Carthage from the time of the Indians through the Civil War to the present. Two local and very diverse women of distinction are represented in the picture. One is Annie Baxter, elected as Jasper County clerk in 1891 (the first woman elected to public office in the United States); the other is Belle Starr, "Queen of the Outlaws."

Belle Starr was born as Myra Maebelle Shirley in 1848. She was the educated daughter of John Shirley, a prosperous Carthage businessman who strongly supported the Confederacy during the Civil War. After her brother Edward was killed by Union troops, Maebelle—an expert rider and crack shot—joined a Confederate outlaw band that included the likes of Frank and Jesse James. After she married Sam Starr, their homestead became a notorious hideout for their infamous outlaw friends. Belle was shot and killed on February 3, 1889.

Just north of the courthouse, at 205 E. Grant Street (the street you followed into town), is the **Civil War Museum**. To reach the museum, stroll east on Third to Grant, and turn left. The museum is in the middle of the block on the left. If you enjoy history, don't miss it.

Civil War Museum

Telephone: (417) 237-7060; Hours: Monday through Saturday, 9 A.M. to 5 P.M.; Sunday, 1 to 5 P.M; Season: Year-round (hours are subject to change); Admission: Free

The focal point of the museum is a huge seven-by-fifteen-foot mural designed by another famous Carthage artist, **Andy Thomas**. The huge portrait portrays not only the military warfare that took place on the square, but also the horror and devastating impact it had on the individuals involved. Note the fearful yet resolute expressions on the faces of the soldiers— on both sides—as they fought to defend their convictions. Available at the desk is a one-page summary of what's happening in the painting.

Among the museum's Civil War artifacts and artwork is a diorama depicting various troop movements. If you would like to learn more about the Battle of Carthage, ask at the desk for a brief description.

When ready to leave the square, head left (if you're parked at the visitor center) and immediately make another left onto Main Street (you'll be heading south). Carthage's historic homes will begin appearing immediately so don't drive too fast. If you picked up the Victorian Homes brochure from the Chambers, or have the cassette, you'll be able to ascertain what architectural styles were used and also learn something about each home's history. **The Hill House**, 1157 Main, is especially striking. Built in 1887 by a local banker, Frank Hill, the chateau-like structure has a multitude of picturesque spires, pinnacles, turrets, and chimneys.

When you reach **Centennial Street**, turn left and travel one block to **Grand Avenue** (the street on which you traveled into town). If you want to take another look at the homes along Grand, turn left and follow it back to the square. From the square, follow the route you just traveled and you'll be back where you are now, at the corner of Centennial and Grand.

The Way Back

From Grand and Centennial, make a right turn and follow Grand all the way (about four miles) to **Interstate 44** (when you come to the stoplight, you'll make a jog and veer left). After reaching I-44, you'll cross over the highway before heading east toward Springfield. It's about sixty-six miles from Carthage to **U.S. 65** in Springfield.

To begin heading south on 65, towards Branson, stay in the right lane as you approach the intersection. It takes about forty-five minutes to travel the forty-five scenic miles back to Branson and **Missouri 76**.

Index